U.S. Department of
Homeland Security

**United States
Coast Guard**

Coast Guard Navigation Standards Manual

COMDTINST M3530.2F
January 2020

U.S. Department of Homeland Security

United States Coast Guard

Commandant
United States Coast Guard

US Coast Guard Stop 7324
2703 Martin Luther King Jr. Ave SE
Washington, DC 20593-7324
Staff Symbol: (CG-7)
Phone: 202-372-2020

COMDTINST M3530.2F
21 JAN 2020

COMMANDANT INSTRUCTION M3530.2F

Subj: COAST GUARD NAVIGATION STANDARDS MANUAL

Ref: (a) United States Coast Guard Regulations 1992, COMDTINST M5000.3 (series)
        (b) Cutter Training and Qualification Manual, COMDTINST M3502.4 (series)
        (c) U.S. Coast Guard Boat Operations and Training (BOAT) Manual, Volume I,
            COMDTINST M16114.32 (series)
        (d) U.S. Coast Guard Boat Operations and Training (BOAT) Manual, Volume II,
            COMDTINST M16114.33 (series)
        (e) U.S. Coast Guard Boat Operations and Training (BOAT) Manual, Volume III,
            COMDTINST M16114.42 (series)
        (f) U.S. Navy Ship Control and Navigation Personnel Qualification Standard (PQS),
            NAVEDTRA 43492 (series)
        (g) Risk Management (RM), COMDTINST 3500.3 (series)
        (h) Cutter Organization Manual, COMDTINST M5400.16 (series)
        (i) Information and Life Cycle Management Manual, COMDTINST M5212.12 (series)
        (j) Procedures for the Preparation and Disposition of Cutter Logs, COMDTINST M3123.12
            (series)
        (k) The Coast Guard Directives System, COMDTINST M5215.6 (series)
        (l) Telecommunication Manual, COMDTINST M2000.3 (series)
        (m) Personnel Qualification Standard (PQS), Coast Guard Navigator

1. <u>PURPOSE</u>. This Manual updates the Coast Guard Navigation Standards for safe navigation of
   vessels. Per Reference (a), unit commanders are responsible for the safe navigation of their vessels
   and/or assigned boats. All Commanding Officers (COs) and Officer-in-Charge (OICs) are required
   to promulgate unit-specific Command Navigation Standards that align with the requirements
   contained in this Manual. Unit-specific Command Navigation Standards must be written broadly
   enough to enable the safe navigation of cutters, cutter boats, and shore-based boats (referred to as

DISTRIBUTION – SDL No.170

	a	b	c	d	e	f	g	h	i	j	k	l	m	n	o	p	q	r	s	t	u	v	w	x	y	z
A	X	X	X	X	X	X	X	X	X	X		X	X	X	X	X	X		X		X	X				
B	X	X	X	X	X	X	X	X	X	X	X	X	X	X	X	X	X	X	X	X	X	X	X	X	X	X
C	X	X	X	X	X	X	X	X	X	X	X	X	X	X	X	X	X	X	X	X	X	X	X	X	X	X
D	X	X	X	X	X	X	X	X	X	X	X	X	X	X	X	X	X	X	X	X	X	X	X	X	X	X
E	X	X	X	X	X	X	X	X	X	X	X	X	X	X	X	X	X	X	X	X	X	X	X			
F																	X	X	X							
G		X	X	X	X																					
H	X	X	X	X	X	X	X																			

NON-STANDARD DISTRIBUTION:

"boats" for this Manual) for a variety of challenging missions across multiple operating areas. However, these Command Navigation Standards must also be specific enough to ensure the precise navigation of these same assets across the full spectrum of conditions that may be encountered.

2. <u>ACTION</u>. All Coast Guard Unit Commanders, COs, OICs, Deputy/Assistant Commandants, and Chiefs of Headquarters staff elements must comply with the provisions of this Manual. Internet release is authorized.

3. <u>DIRECTIVES AFFECTED</u>. Coast Guard Navigation Standards, COMDTINST M3530.2E and Nautical Chart and Publication Allowance for Cutters, COMDTINST M3140.5B, are cancelled.

4. <u>DISCUSSION</u>.

   a. Navigation is a critical and fundamental competency for all underway operations. This Manual assists CO/OICs and Navigators in carrying out their responsibilities outlined in Reference (a), and complements References (b) through (l). It also provides uniform standards and guidance to ensure the navigational accuracy and safety of Coast Guard cutters, boats, and their crews during operations.

   b. This Manual leverages the capabilities provided by electronic navigation systems found on cutters, cutter boats, and boats while retaining the capability to conduct traditional forms of navigation if, and when, electronic means of navigation are not available.

   c. Analysis of operational mishaps and studies have shown that risks associated with navigation can be systematically controlled by:

      (1) Strong knowledge and skills in navigation fundamentals, doctrine, and techniques.

      (2) Preventing accumulation of errors in the flow of information.

      (3) Verifying vessel position using all available means.

      (4) Strong knowledge regarding the structure, capabilities, and limitations of electronic charting and Global Positioning System (GPS) data.

      (5) Compliance with established navigational procedures.

   d. Documents that drive and guide navigation standards and decisions to ensure safe navigation of Coast Guard cutters and boats span from the international to the unit level and include, but are not limited to, the list and examples provided below. Awareness and knowledge of these documents contribute to the development of Command Navigation Standards and safe navigation of Coast Guard cutters and boats.

      (1) International Level. International consensus standards provide industry standards for systems design, performance, and evaluation. Consensus standards are particularly applicable to electronic navigation. Examples include:

(a) Navigation Standards established by the International Maritime Organization (IMO) Maritime Safety Committee.

(b) Standards from the International Association of Marine Aids to Navigation and Lighthouse Authorities (IALA) concerning items such as the IALA Maritime Buoyage System and other navigation guidance.

(2) Federal Level.

(a) Laws and Regulations. Code of Federal Regulations (CFR): Title 33 – Navigation and Navigable Waters, specifies navigation requirements for private, commercial, and public vessels.

(b) Doctrine. Includes publications by the National Geospatial-Intelligence Agency (NGA) and other governmental sources (e.g., The American Practical Navigator (Bowditch), Pub 9). These documents contain the cumulative wealth of generations of seagoing professionals and serve as the foundation of navigation knowledge and skills.

(3) Organization/Program Level.

(a) Publications at the Coast Guard organizational and program levels include policy, doctrine, and tactics, techniques, and procedures (TTP). Reference (k) further defines these publication types, their relationships to each other, and their various audiences.

(b) The Office of Cutter Forces, Commandant (CG-751), and the Office of Boat Forces, Commandant (CG-731), provide organizational guidance for cutter and boat acquisition, navigation, and maneuvering in the form of requirements, policy, doctrine, and TTP.

(4) Unit Level. Provides local policy, doctrine, and TTP that amplify procedures required to ensure compliance with national and program policies and doctrine.

5. DISCLAIMER. This guidance is not a substitute for applicable legal requirements, nor is it itself a rule. It is intended to provide guidance for Coast Guard personnel and is not intended to, nor does it, impose legally binding requirements on any party outside the Coast Guard.

6. MAJOR CHANGES.

a. Previous Navigation Modes were defined as I, II, or III. These were updated/consolidated into new definitions for Automated Plotting and Manual Plotting Navigation Modes.

b. Paper chart correction requirements were updated for the Manual Plotting Mode.

c. The requirement for currently corrected paper charts on boats was changed to requiring a portfolio of currently corrected master paper charts onboard the unit.

  d. Seaman's eye was included as an acceptable means of secondary navigation when necessary.

  e. Navigational and paper chart carriage requirements were clarified, or changed, for cutter boats.

  f. Voyage Planning and Voyage Monitoring terms were introduced in order to better align with current International Maritime Organization (IMO) terminology.

  g. Chapters were added/combined/updated.

   (1) Separate Chapters were added for cutter and boat specific information.

   (2) Content from previous Chapters (Navigation Planning and Briefs, Electronic Navigation, and Paper Navigation) was moved into cutter and boat specific Chapters.

   (3) A Chapter was added for Navigation Fundamentals, which incorporates general doctrine from previous Chapters.

   (4) A short Chapter was added for Completely Paperless Chart Navigation in order to prepare for future changes.

  h. Enclosures were updated/added.

   (1) A Voyage Planning References and Resources Enclosure was added.

   (2) A Boat Navigation Kit Outfit Enclosure was added.

   (3) Enclosure (9), Cutter Logs and Records, was updated to change the requirement to locally maintain getting underway and entering port/restricted waters checklists from 90 days to 30 days.

7. ENVIRONMENTAL ASPECT AND IMPACT CONSIDERATIONS.

  a. The development of this Manual and the general policies contained within it have been thoroughly reviewed by the originating office in conjunction with the Office of Environmental Management, Commandant (CG-47). This Manual is categorically excluded under current Department of Homeland Security (DHS) categorical exclusion DHS (CATEX) A3 from further environmental analysis in accordance with the U.S. Coast Guard Environmental Planning Policy, COMDTINST 5090.1 and the Environmental Planning (EP) Implementing Procedures (IP).

  b. This Manual will not have any of the following: significant cumulative impacts on the human environment; substantial controversy or substantial change to existing environmental conditions; or inconsistencies with any Federal, State, or local laws or administrative determinations relating to the environment. All future specific actions resulting from the general policy in this Manual must be individually evaluated for compliance with the National Environmental Policy Act (NEPA) and Environmental Effects Abroad of Major

Federal Actions, Executive Order 12114, Department of Homeland Security (DHS) NEPA policy, Coast Guard Environmental Planning policy, and compliance with all other applicable environmental mandates.

8. <u>DISTRIBUTION</u>. No paper distribution will be made of this Manual. An electronic version will be located on the following Commandant (CG-612) web sites. CGPortal: https://cg.portal.uscg.mil/library/directives/SitePages/Home.aspx and the Internet: http://www.dcms.uscg.mil/directives.

9. <u>RECORDS MANAGEMENT CONSIDERATIONS</u>. This Manual has been thoroughly reviewed during the directives clearance process, and it has been determined there are no further records scheduling requirements, in accordance with Federal Records Act, 44 U.S.C. 3101 et seq., National Archives and Records Administration (NARA) requirements, and Information and Life Cycle Management Manual, COMDTINST M5212.12 (series). This policy does not create significant or substantial change to existing records management requirements.

10. <u>FORMS/REPORTS</u>. The forms referenced in this Manual are available in USCG Electronic Forms on the Standard Workstation or on the Internet: https://www.dcms.uscg.mil/forms/; and CG Portal https://cg.portal.uscg.mil/library/forms/SitePages/Home.aspx. Chief of Naval Operations (OPNAV) Forms are available here: https://forms.documentservices.dla.mil/process/.

11. <u>REQUEST FOR CHANGES</u>. Commandants (CG-751) and (CG-731) will coordinate changes to this Manual. This Manual is under continual review and will be updated as necessary. Time-sensitive amendments will be promulgated via message, pending their inclusion in the next change. All users are urged to provide recommendations for improvement to this Manual via the chain of command.

MATTHEW W. SIBLEY /s/
Rear Admiral, U.S. Coast Guard
Assistant Commandant for Capability

RECORD OF CHANGES			
CHANGE NUMBER	DATE OF CHANGE	DATE ENTERED	BY WHOM ENTERED

TABLE OF CONTENTS

CHAPTER 1. COMMAND RESPONSIBILITIES AND TRAINING 1-1

A. General...1-1
B. Program Responsibility..1-1
C. Navigator Requirements for Cutters and Shore-Based Boat Units....................................1-1
D. Command Responsibilities for all Units..1-1
E. Additional Command Responsibilities for Cutters 1-1
F. Additional Command Responsibilities for Boats 1-2
G. Training..1-2

CHAPTER 2. NAVIGATION FUNDAMENTALS 2-1

A. General...2-1
B. Navigation Fundamentals 2-1
C. Modes of Navigation..2-1
D. Seaman's Eye 2-1
E. Overview of Navigation...2-1
F. Chart Types 2-2
G. Approved Electronic Chart Hierarchy 2-3
H. Chart Correction and Updating..2-4
I. Fixing a Vessel's Position 2-4
J. Dead Reckoning...2-5
K. Challenges Inherent to Boat and Cutter Boat Navigation...2-6
L. The Role of Voyage Planning and Voyage Monitoring as Part of the Process of Navigation 2-7
M. The Basics of Electronic Navigation Systems 2-8
N. Satellite Navigation Systems 2-10

CHAPTER 3. CUTTER NAVIGATION REQUIREMENTS...3-1

A. Introduction..3-1
B. Voyage Planning Requirements...3-1
C. Voyage Monitoring Requirements...3-6
D. Electronic Navigation Requirements 3-8
E. Paper Chart Navigation Requirements...3-10
F. Cutter Boat Specific Navigation Requirements 3-11

CHAPTER 4. SHORE-BASED BOAT NAVIGATION REQUIREMENTS.........................4-1

A. Introduction..4-1
B. Voyage Planning Requirements...4-1
C. Voyage Monitoring Requirements...4-4
D. Electronic Navigation Requirements 4-5
E. Paper Chart Navigation Requirements...4-6

CHAPTER 5. COMMAND NAVIGATION STANDARDS CONTENT REQUIREMENTS 5-1

A. General...5-1
B. Command Navigation Standards Content Requirements 5-1

CHAPTER 6. COMPLETELY PAPERLESS CHART NAVIGATION 6-1

A. Background/Commercial Chart Carriage Requirements 6-1
B. Sun-setting of Raster/Paper Charts 6-1
C. Authorized Paperless Coast Guard Vessels 6-1

LIST OF TABLES

Table 2-1: Primary Modes of Navigation 2-1
Table 2-2: Electronic Chart Hierarchy for Data Accuracy 2-3
Table 2-3: Six Rules for Dead Reckoning 2-6
Table 3-1: Cutter Navigational Information 3-1
Table 3-2: Cutter Navigation Brief Items 3-5
Table 3-3: Cutter Navigation Mode Requirements 3-6
Table 3-4: Cutter Boat Navigational and Voyage Planning Information 3-11
Table 3-5: Cutter Boat Crew Brief Items..3-13
Table 4-1: Boat Crew Brief Items...4-3
Table 4-2: Boat Navigation Mode Requirements 4-4
Table 5-1: Command Navigation Standards Content Requirements...............................5-1

LIST OF FIGURES

Figure 2-1: Navigational Draft...2-7

ENCLOSURES

(1) LIST OF ACRONYMS
(2) ANCHORING
(3) CELESTIAL NAVIGATION
(4) NAVIGATION TEAMS
(5) LINE HANDLING COMMANDS
(6) HELM COMMANDS
(7) NAVIGATION PLOTTING SYMBOLS
(8) GPS OUTAGE REPORTING
(9) CUTTER LOGS AND RECORDS
(10) SAMPLE CUTTER GETTING UNDERWAY CHECKLIST
(11) SAMPLE CUTTER ENTERING PORT/APPROACHING RESTRICTED WATERS CHECKLIST
(12) VOYAGE PLANNING REFERENCES AND RESOURCES
(13) BOAT/CUTTER BOAT NAVIGATION KIT OUTFIT LIST

CHAPTER 1. **COMMAND RESPONSIBILITIES AND TRAINING**

A. <u>General</u>. This Chapter outlines navigation responsibilities for Coast Guard cutters and Boat Forces units.

B. <u>Program Responsibility</u>. Commandant (CG-751) is responsible for cutter and cutter boat navigation programs. Commandant (CG-731) is responsible for shore-based boat navigation programs (shore-based boats are referred to as just "boats" for this Manual). Commandant (CG-761) is responsible for Coast Guard electronic navigation capabilities for all units.

C. <u>Navigator Requirements for Cutters and Shore-Based Boat Units</u>.

1. <u>Cutters</u>: All cutters must designate a Navigator in accordance with Reference (a). The Navigator must complete Reference (f), and be certified by the CO/OIC. Upon promulgation of Reference (m), navigators can no longer be qualified using Reference (f). Designated Navigators should be an experienced underway OOD who possesses the requisite maturity, judgment, training, and navigational proficiency required to fill this position. It is also recommended that enlisted Navigators attend the Senior Bridge Resource Management course. Reference (f) is available on the Cutter Forces website: https://cg.portal.uscg.mil/units/cg751/SitePages/PQS.aspx.

2. <u>Shore-Based Boat Units</u>: All shore based units must designate a Navigation Petty Officer in accordance with Reference (c). Navigation Petty Officers must be certified by the CO/OIC and be an experienced coxswain who has the navigational proficiency in electronic navigation systems, nautical charts, and manual plotting methods. Reference (c) is available on the Boat Forces website at https://cg.portal.uscg.mil/units/cg731/SitePages/Home.aspx.

D. <u>Command Responsibilities for all Units</u>.

1. Ensure compliance with the provisions of this Manual. COs/OICs of units that regularly operate in the western rivers and/or inland waters must tailor the requirements of this Manual to their unique areas of responsibility, missions, navigation techniques, and the lack of accurate charting as appropriate, to ensure maximum compliance with the requirements contained in this Manual in their Command Navigation Standards.

2. Promulgate Command Navigation Standards within 90 days of assuming command. Prior Command Navigation Standards remain in effect until superseded.

3. Assign, train, and certify navigation personnel in accordance with References (a) through (h), as appropriate.

4. Incorporate the principles of effective risk management into navigational planning in accordance with Reference (g). Commands can tailor the risk assessment process to be consistent with the complexity of the specific mission, but must not omit any step in the process.

E. <u>Additional Command Responsibilities for Cutters</u>.

1. Ensure a primary navigation team is trained and proficient. See Enclosure (4) for more information.

2. For cutters so equipped, maintain crew proficiency in anchoring in accordance with Reference (b). See Enclosure (2) for more information.

3. Maintain crew proficiency in celestial navigation for WMSP, WAGB, WMSL, WHEC, WMSM, WMEC, WIX, and D14/D17 WLB class cutters. See Enclosure (3) for more information.

4. For cutters with a Combat Information Center (CIC), ensure a secondary navigation team (CIC) is trained, proficient, and capable of fulfilling primary navigation team duties when required. See Enclosure (4) for more information.

5. Fully understand all modes of operation for the cutter (e.g. dynamic positioning modes, various propulsion configurations such as CODAG, gas turbine, etc.) and impacts of shifting between modes during restricted waters transits on the cutter's maneuverability and safe navigation.

F. Additional Command Responsibilities for Boats.

1. Ensure boat crews are trained to provide navigation support functions to the Coxswain per Reference (d).

2. Develop their coxswains' ability to navigate by seaman's eye through extensive Area of Responsibility (AOR) familiarization and boat platform knowledge.

G. Training. Maintaining proficiency of navigation skills through training and practice is critical to safe navigation. Additionally, a thorough understanding of navigation fundamentals is essential to the proper operation of installed navigational equipment and sensors, understanding their limitations, and reducing the risk presented by over reliance on any single source of information. CO/OICs must:

1. Conduct navigation exercises in accordance with References (b) and (d).

2. Maintain proficiency in basic navigation skills, including:

   a. Preparedness to operate in all modes of navigation.

   b. Operation of installed charting system(s), radar, and sensors.

   c. Emergency transition from Automated Plotting Mode to Manual Plotting Mode and, following restoration of Automated Plotting Mode capability, the transition back to Automated Plotting Mode.

   d. Celestial navigation for those cutter classes required to maintain proficiency in this type of navigation. See Enclosure (3).

   e.   Piloting by seaman's eye.

3. Consider the use of full mission simulation facilities to provide training in higher risk scenarios. Simulation training should prioritize training of navigation doctrine over specific equipment operation.

4. Ensure training integrates Bridge Resource Management in accordance with Reference (g).

5. In addition to requirements in References (b) through (f), when qualifying CO/OIC designated members responsible for safe cutter/boat navigation, ensure they understand the following:

   a.   The approved configuration of the installed Coast Guard eNav system and indicators that the system capabilities are not performing as designed.

   b.   Quality and limitations of electronic charts used in the eNav system.

   c.   Voyage planning and voyage monitoring capabilities and procedures.

   d.   Manual positioning procedures.

   e.   Alarms or indications regarding displayed information or malfunctions.

   f.   The risks associated with over reliance on a single source of vessel positioning data, such as AIS, GPS, radar, or navigation aids, for safe navigation and collision avoidance.

6. Ensure that current and prospective personnel attend mandated navigation Class "C" school navigation-related courses in accordance with the appropriate cutter Master Training List (MTL) and Reference (b).

CHAPTER 2.   NAVIGATION FUNDAMENTALS

A. <u>General</u>. This Chapter contains a basic description of navigation fundamentals. Later Chapters establish navigational requirements, which are based on the fundamentals discussed in this Chapter.

B. <u>Navigation Fundamentals</u>. Current Coast Guard afloat navigation is primarily conducted by electronic means. Navigation proficiency requires an understanding of the underlying electronic system, as well as the inputs used by the system to generate the display seen by the operator. While electronic navigation has proven very reliable, operators must always be proficient with the traditional navigation principles used by the electronic system, in order to validate/evaluate what is being displayed to them. Prudent Coast Guard afloat navigation personnel must have the ability to correlate all available means of navigational information, and not just blindly follow the electronic display.

C. <u>Modes of Navigation</u>. Many electronic navigation systems can be used in an automated mode or a manual mode using manual inputs to determine vessel position if a primary positioning source fails or is disrupted. In addition, the Coast Guard still recognizes, practices, and uses traditional navigation techniques (including paper charts or other means such as visual lines of position and radar ranges) and celestial navigation. The two modes of primary navigation are summarized in the table below.

Navigation Mode	Definition	Position Source
Automated Plotting	Installed eNav system, with automatic positioning input, used as primary means of navigation.	Automatic Input
Manual Plotting	Installed eNav system, with manual positioning input, used as primary means of navigation. Or, Traditional paper navigation used as primary means of navigation, usually due to eNav failure. Planned use of paper navigation is also done for proficiency and training or when there is a lack of electronic chart availability.	Manual Input

Table 2-1: Primary Modes of Navigation

D. <u>Seaman's Eye</u>. Seaman's eye is defined as navigation based on an extensive knowledge of the local area to include aids to navigation, terrestrial landmarks, and depth contours. Seaman's eye, coupled with all other available navigational tools, can be used by Coast Guard boat coxswains as a primary method of boat navigation and to maintain the situational awareness of the boat's position. For cutters, seaman's eye can correlate what is being displayed on electronic navigation systems with what is being observed visually.

E. <u>Overview of Navigation</u>. Regardless of the mode of navigation, the basic process for navigation is the same. Only the method and medium upon which positional information is plotted, viewed, and evaluated varies depending on the mode of navigation in use. The following Paragraphs provide an overview of the basic process of navigation.

1. <u>Cartography and Nautical Charts</u>. The process of navigation begins with an understanding of cartography and nautical charts. Users must understand the type of chart projection in use and how the scale of the chart in use impacts the user's ability to see details in depth contours, soundings, obstructions, navigational aids, and other chart information. Users must also understand the chart datum and be aware of the age of soundings. Whether using paper or electronic charts, users should always utilize the largest scale chart available for the area in which they are operating.

2. <u>Chart Plotting Symbology</u>. Navigation personnel must be well versed in chart plotting symbology for both paper and electronic charts. Based on the type of electronic chart or electronic navigation in use, there may be slight differences in chart symbology and display.

3. <u>Use all Available Tools</u>. The resources available to navigate vary by individual vessel platform. For boats that have limited electronics or tools for navigation, there will be increased reliance on the use of seaman's eye for navigation. Regardless, all available means for navigation must be used to the maximum extent possible.

4. <u>Process of Navigation</u>. The basic process of navigation is the same for cutters and boats. It begins with a thorough knowledge of plotting and labeling tracklines, using dead reckoning, turn bearings and ranges, plotting visual and electronic fixes, understanding danger bearings and ranges, and how to use and correct both paper and electronic charts. Then, using a known or estimated starting point, the process of navigation utilizes dead reckoning to estimate a vessel's expected position along a known trackline. At regular intervals, the vessel's position is fixed and compared to the dead reckoning position to determine the effects of current, wind, and other external elements on the intended track. This enables navigation personnel to adjust the intended track to compensate for these external forces and ensure the safe navigation of the vessel. Electronic navigation systems perform this same process, continually and automatically, and fuse in additional inputs from other onboard equipment, to provide the user with more situational awareness of their navigational situation.

F. <u>Chart Types</u>.

1. <u>Electronic Charts</u>. There are two general types of electronic charts: vector and raster. Both vector and raster chart data have inherent limitations. Vector charts are the preferred electronic chart type with Coast Guard eNav systems.

   a. <u>Vector Charts</u>. These charts include Electronic Navigation Charts (ENC), Inland Electronic Navigation Charts (IENC), and Digital Nautical Charts (DNC). Vector charts consist of points, lines, and area data that represent real world objects and are stored as a separate data file that can be queried by chart users. They also allow the electronic navigation system to test each object for user-defined grounding or height alarms. Vector charts also allow users to hide or display certain chart objects based on zoom level and operator preference.

   b. <u>Raster Charts</u>. Each paper chart has a corresponding raster chart that is its digital image equivalent. Raster charts are merely a scanned image of a chart. Since it is not "layered", users cannot adjust filters, apply corrections, set grounding or height alarms, or query raster chart data for amplifying information on object or notes.

2. Paper Charts. Paper charts are supplied through government sources such as the National Geospatial-Intelligence Agency (NGA), the Defense Logistics Agency (DLA), or purchased locally from approved chart vendors who meet the chart printing requirements. While several different types of chart projections exist and contain inherent distortions, most paper charts are produced using a Mercator projection.

G. Approved Electronic Chart Hierarchy. Table 2-2 shows the Coast Guard's approved hierarchy of electronic charts based on data accuracy. Additional information for each chart type is listed below.

Electronic Chart Hierarchy for Data Accuracy
1. Official ENC/USACE IENC
2. NGA DNC
3. Official RNC
4. Commercial Vector Chart
5. Commercial Raster Charts

Table 2-2: Electronic Chart Hierarchy for Data Accuracy

1. Electronic Navigational Charts (ENC). Government-authorized hydrographic offices (NOAA) produce and issue official ENCs. ENCs use US Chart 1 symbology. Updates are available at: http://www.charts.noaa.gov/ENCs/ENCs.shtml.

2. Inland Electronic Navigational Charts (IENC). US Army Corps of Engineers (USACE) produces and issues IENCs, basing them on the ENC format with data that conforms to the Inland ENC Harmonization Group (IEHG) standard. IENC must meet the issuing criteria detailed above for ENCs. These charts cover the Western Rivers and have additional symbols specific to this region not found on other ENCs. Updates are available at: http://navigation.usace.army.mil/Survey/InlandCharts.

3. Digital Nautical Charts (DNC). NGA produces and issues DNCs for use outside of US waters, where NOAA does not have ENC coverage. NGA is in the process of converting DNCs to the ENC format, but they have not been released yet. NGA publishes DNCs in general, coastal, approach, and harbor libraries. NGA updates DNCs monthly, and users can download DNCs directly from NGA's website. However, as these charts rely on other country's hydrographic data, the data on these charts is only as reliable as the standards set by the host country's Hydrographic Office. DNCs present data using NGA's Geospatial Symbols for Digital Displays, which corresponds to the International Hydrographic Organization (IHO) Electronic Chart Display and Information System (ECDIS) Presentation Library and IHO International Chart 1. NGA DNC updates are available at: https://www.geointel.nga.mil/products/dnc/#updated. NGA Registration is at: https://pki.geointel.nga.mil/servlet/RegistrationForm.

4. Raster Navigational Charts (RNC). Government-authorized hydrographic offices produce and issue RNCs. The chart name usually aligns with the equivalent paper chart. NOAA's RNCs use

US Chart 1 symbology. RNCs other than NOAA's RNCs use symbols based on International Chart 1 and contain variants as determined by the producer. Updates are available at: http://www.charts.noaa.gov/RNCs/RNCs.shtml. NOAA is phasing out production of paper and raster charts. Users should note that raster products still in existence may not be updated as frequently, or may have only been updated with those corrections listed in the LNM and some updates otherwise deemed as "critical." RNC products will not have as up to date hydrographic data as is available with ENC.

H. <u>Chart Correction and Updating</u>. Notice to Mariners (NTM) and Local Notice to Mariners (LNM) provide needed chart correction updates. Paper chart corrections need to be manually plotted on the chart. A record of the updates applied to a paper chart are listed on a mariner's cross, located on the chart. For electronic charts, the Coast Guard has contractual agreements in place to provide units with a periodic update to both cutter and boat electronic charting systems. Some electronic charts may also be updated manually.

I. <u>Fixing a Vessel's Position</u>. The equipment available to fix a vessel's position varies by platform, but the process is the same. Electronic navigation systems provide continual and near-real time fix positions. However, navigation personnel must understand and be proficient in the use of all available means to fix their position, especially if or when, installed electronic systems fail or become unreliable. This Section discusses the types of fixes that may be used and the basic processes for obtaining a fix.

1. <u>The Process of Fixing a Vessel's Position</u>. Fixing a vessel's position uses fixed, terrestrial, or celestial objects to generate lines of position (LOPs) and/or radar ranges. These LOPs or radar ranges must be taken as simultaneously as possible to ensure accuracy and must be adjusted as required to account for computed errors (e.g. gyro error, repeater errors, or radar range errors). These LOPs and radar ranges are then entered into an electronic navigation system or plotted on a paper chart. The intersection of LOPs and/or radar ranges at a singular point is the vessel's "fixed" position at the time of observation. A position may also be fixed when installed positioning equipment that provides latitude and longitude is plotted on an electronic or paper chart. Enclosure (7) contains standard fix symbology used in the Coast Guard. From this fixed position, navigation personnel can determine the effects of external forces on their vessel, compensate accordingly, create new dead reckoning plots, and ensure the safe navigation of their vessel. For vessels with integrated navigation systems, overlaying the radar image on the electronic chart can also be used as a form of fixing a vessel's position. Based on the equipment and process used to fix a position, a fix may be classified as one of the following:

   a. Electronic Fix. The use of installed electronic equipment to develop a position fix includes:

      (1) Latitude and longitude provided by installed positioning equipment.

      (2) The common intersection of three or more radar ranges, or a combination of visual LOPs and radar ranges, obtained from simultaneous observations, is an electronic fix.

   b. <u>Visual Fix</u>. The common intersection of three or more lines of position at a common point obtained from simultaneous observations. (Lines of position from celestial bodies, if properly advanced from the time of observation, may also be included, despite not being simultaneous observations.)

    c. <u>Running Fix</u>. Used when limited objects are available for taking LOPs and the vessel remains on a consistent course. This type of fix advances or retires a LOP taken to the same object at two different times to fix the vessel's position

2. <u>Verify Vessel Position</u>. Radar/chart matching involves verifying the vessel's position with the installed eNav system and the radar to match features that appear on both (e.g. Radar overlay feature on eNav System). The use of a fathometer to match observed depth with charted depth is also a means of verification.

3. <u>Evaluate Position Fixes</u>. Whether a fix is taken by visual or electronic means, it must be evaluated. This means the fix must be analyzed with due regard to its accuracy, relation to the vessel's intended track, proximity of shoal water or other navigational hazards, environmental conditions and their effect on a vessel's intended track, and any other situation dependent factors that must be considered for safe navigation. The following Paragraphs describe some of the external factors that may influence a vessel's position relative to its intended track:

    a. <u>Set and Drift</u>. Set and Drift is the cumulative effect of wind, tide, and current on a vessel's movement through the water. Set is the direction, (True or Magnetic degrees), these cumulative influences have moved the vessel towards, relative to the vessel's expected position. Drift is how these cumulative influences have affected the planned speed of the vessel. Navigation personnel can adjust actual courses and speeds to counteract the cumulative influences of Set and Drift to ensure the planned direction and speed of the vessel is achieved.

    b. <u>Vessel Advance and Transfer</u>. Especially during or after executing a turn, deviations from intended track and track speed may occur from the turning characteristics of the vessel. There are many factors that influence a vessel's advance and transfer that must be accounted for in the process of navigation. Advance is the distance along the vessel's current track it will travel during a turn. Transfer is the distance perpendicular, or the slide, a vessel will experience as it travels through a turn. Most electronic navigation systems enable operators to input a vessel's tactical data into the system for the purposes of computed wheel over points, slide lines, or turn points. This computation must be performed manually on paper charts.

    c. <u>Plotting Errors</u>. Fix evaluation must also account for the potential for plotting errors and inaccuracies with individual LOPs or radar ranges in use due to non-simultaneous observations or inaccuracies with how the LOP or radar range was determined. Consistent issues with individual objects or radar ranges may necessitate changing the object or radar range used for navigation.

J. <u>Dead Reckoning</u>. Both electronic and paper chart navigation utilize dead reckoning, which is the process of plotting a course from a known position, at a given speed and duration of time, to determine a vessel's anticipated or estimated position along a trackline. When compared to the vessel's known or fixed position at a specific time, it enables personnel to determine the effect of external influences, such as wind, current, and tide on a vessel's motion. The following table lists general rules for constructing and maintaining a dead reckoning plot.

Six Rules for Dead Reckoning
1. Plot a new DR position at least every hour on the hour.
2. Plot a new DR position at every course change.
3. Plot a new DR position at every speed change.
4. Plot a new DR position after each fix or running fix.
5. Plot a new DR position when obtaining a single line of position.
6. Plot a new course line from each fix or running fix.

Table 2-3: Six Rules for Dead Reckoning

K. Challenges Inherent to Boat and Cutter Boat Navigation. The navigation process described above is inherently more challenging for Coast Guard boats due to limited availability of navigation equipment as well as limited space to conduct navigation. While installed electronic navigation systems on Coast Guard boats are highly reliable, boat coxswains must be practiced and ready to use other means to safely navigate in case these systems fail. The following Paragraphs describe secondary processes boat coxswains (and in some cases, cutter boat coxswains) can use to navigate their platforms:

1. Manual Plotting. In the event of a failure of a required input to a boat's electronic navigation system, positions from installed positioning receivers can be plotted on a paper chart. This method can be especially challenging for open construction boats, as paper charts will be exposed to the elements limiting the practicality of this method of boat navigation for extended periods.

2. Use of Radar Ranges. Most Coast Guard boats have installed radar systems. If there is a failure of the primary positioning source in an installed electronic navigation system, radar ranges can be obtained, plotted, and used for navigation. If the boat's installed electronic system permits the use of manually inputted radar ranges, this is the preferred process for boat navigation following a failure of the installed electronic navigation system. Otherwise, boat coxswains should obtain and plot radar ranges on paper charts to the extent possible based on the boat platform in use.

3. Use of Danger Ranges and Soundings. When unable to take a fix or maintain an active plot of a boat's position during a transit, boat coxswains can use danger ranges and soundings to assist with safe boat navigation. While not a fix, determining and using danger ranges and soundings can help estimate a boat's position relative to known hazards or the boundaries of a navigational channel. The use danger ranges and soundings requires active monitoring of the radar or depth sounder by the boat coxswain or another boat crewman.

4. Use of Seaman's Eye. In some cases, the use of seaman's eye may be the most prudent form of navigation to estimate position without navigational instruments. An estimated position can be determined by utilizing distances and angles obtained from instinctive knowledge and experience. Seaman's eye as a tool and form of navigation takes time and practice, to develop proficiency. Navigating by seaman's eye requires significant afloat competence, including the

ability to collate all available inputs in a given situation and combine that with intimate knowledge of boat handling characteristics to then take a course of action that demonstrates prudent judgment and seamanship.

L. The Role of Voyage Planning and Voyage Monitoring as Part of the Process of Navigation. The International Maritime Organization uses the terms Voyage Planning and Voyage Monitoring as a part of the overall process of navigation. The development of a voyage plan, as well as the close and continuous monitoring of the vessel's progress and position during the execution of such a plan (voyage monitoring), are essential to safe and efficient navigation.

1. Voyage Planning. Voyage planning encompasses the development of long and short-term plans as well as contingency plans for a particular transit. It is the process of detailed planning of the entire voyage including port calls or stops along the way. Command Navigation Standards, Standing Orders, operational bills, and navigation checklists are planning tools that support safe and successful navigation. These planning tools help guide the short-term plans that commands can tailor to meet the unique requirements of each operation. Short-term plans include chart preparations as well as navigation and boat crew briefs. These short-term plans could be very elaborate, consisting of complete tracklines, piloting procedure discussions, and extensive briefs regarding planned operations or they may simply be a brief to the crew before launching a boat. Voyage planning references and resources are provided in Enclosure (12).

   a. Navigational Draft. Navigational Draft is defined as a depth of water that serves as the threshold for safe operations, as determined be the CO/OIC. Navigational Draft is calculated by adding the total vessel draft (including appendages in displacement mode) with a safety margin. The safety margin ensures timely warning and response prior to a portion of the vessel making contact with the bottom. Accounting for navigational draft is a critical piece of the voyage planning process to ensure safe navigation.

   b. Navigational Draft Illustration. The following graphic illustrates Navigational Draft.

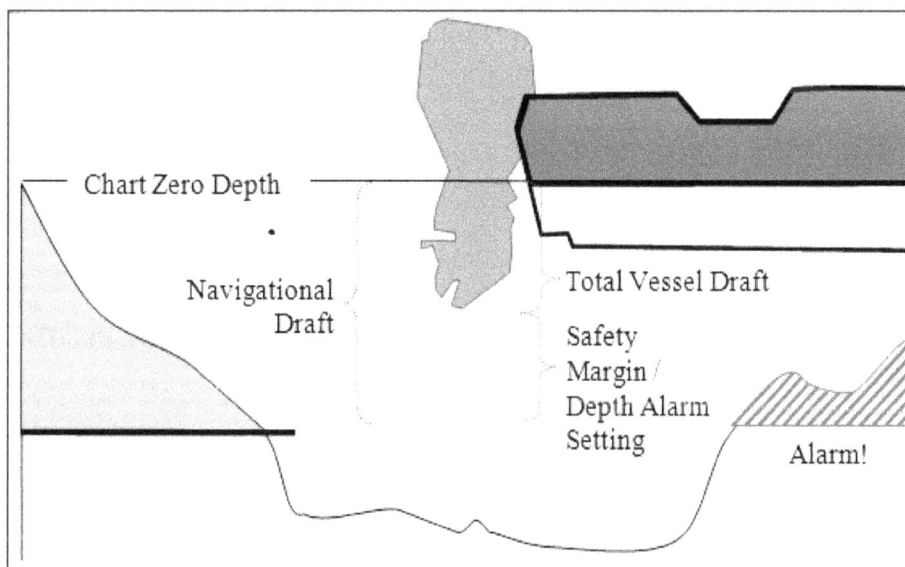

Figure 2-1: Navigational Draft

2. Voyage Monitoring. Voyage monitoring is the process of continuously monitoring a vessel's planned voyage to ensure the plan is followed. Voyage monitoring includes establishing procedures for making changes to the established voyage plan and making appropriate notifications when changes are required.

M. The Basics of Electronic Navigation Systems. Coast Guard installed electronic navigation systems vary in complexity and in their ability to mitigate navigational risk. System capabilities range from display of a vessel's position on an approved electronic chart to systems that integrate all navigation sensors. On more modern platforms, electronic navigation systems also interface with external tactical systems. Alarms from sensors and from chart data can warn of potentially dangerous situations well in advance. Electronic navigation systems do not replace the process of navigation, but their ability to integrate real-time position information with an electronic chart display allows vessels to have an immediate assessment of position. However, over reliance on electronic navigation systems can cause tunnel vision or ignorance of fundamental signs of danger. To prevent this, it is critical to understand system limitations and use foundational navigation skills to properly prepare these systems and detect errors.

1. Approved Coast Guard Electronic Navigation Systems (eNav). Commandant (CG-751) maintains a list of approved Coast Guard electronic navigation systems and additional information to support unit electronic navigation capabilities at the Cutter Forces website https://cg.portal.uscg.mil/units/cg751/NAV/Forms/AllItems.aspx.

2. System Configuration and Settings. When using electronic navigation systems for navigation, it is critical to ensure cutter and boat personnel responsible for navigation have a thorough understanding of the system's operation and functional capabilities as it is easy for operators to manipulate the system settings, configurations, or display to function against safe navigation practices, thereby increasing risk to the cutter or boat. Ensuring correct system inputs, such as cutter or boat draft information and masthead height, are critical to effective system operation.

3. Electronic Navigation Display Objects. Depending on the chart type in use, electronic navigation systems allow operators to display certain chart information in layers. Typically, this chart information falls into one of three categories.

   a. Display Base. The chart content that cannot be removed from the display. This represents the minimum set of information and is not intended to be sufficient for navigation. Shallow water, safety contour, and isolated hazards to navigation are included in the display base depending on the cutter or boat information entered into the eNav system.

   b. Standard Display. The minimum information required for display during route planning and route monitoring for safe navigation of the vessel.

   c. All Other Information. Other information, in addition to the standard display, to be shown individually (by class) on demand, to ensure safe navigation of specific operating areas/ conditions.

4. Use of System Profiles. Many electronic navigation systems have the capability to set, save, and lock operator settings in a profile. This allows transition from one Navigation Zone/Area to

another quickly and reliably, with the same set of settings applied consistently. For instance, the dead reckoning interval and chart features displayed onscreen vary depending on the navigational zone/area. Changing profiles applies all of the settings within the electronic navigation system with one action. It is also possible (and recommended) for units to create standard profiles for vessel-specific evolutions (e.g., anchoring, or working a buoy on the port or starboard side that changes the safety-checking region accordingly). If the Scalable Integrated Navigation System (SINS) package for a boat platform allows for the use of system profiles, boat units should establish and use system profiles for each of the Navigation Zones/Areas in their AOR.

5. Electronic Chart Data Scaling.

   a. Viewing. Electronic chart data is most accurate when displayed at its source scale. Scaling/zooming in, or out, distorts the visually perceived relative distance between chart objects. However, some systems display an overscale pattern if outside its source scale. In addition, cursor-indicated positions for charted features vary when scaling the chart.

   b. Display Matching. Display matching ensures displayed information is consistently oriented to the viewer, thereby preventing errors in interpretation.

      (1) When the system displays radar and electronic chart data together in overlay mode, the display must match in scale, orientation, and projection. For example, scaling out the radar to 24 NM when the electronic chart scale is at 3 NM can cause misinterpretations.

      (2) Display Matching and Chart Matching are not the same; Chart Matching is a means of fix verification, Display Matching is not.

6. Alarms. Electronic navigation systems have many alarms available to the operator that provide valuable information only if they are properly configured for the prevailing navigational situation. Too few alarms increase the risk to the safe navigation of the vessel. However, setting too many alarms creates distractions and makes it difficult, or impossible, to identify risk to the safe navigation of the vessel.

   a. Alarm Hierarchy. Generally, Coast Guard electronic navigation systems have three alarm levels as described below. For units with eNav systems that do not use this three-alarm hierarchy, ensure operators know the corresponding alarm levels and functions for the eNav system in use.

      (1) Danger. The system produces a continuous audible alarm and flashes red. Danger alarms alert the user to issues that require immediate attention.

      (2) Warning. The system produces a brief audible alarm and flashes yellow. Warning alarms alert the user to issues that, if left uncorrected, could compromise navigational safety.

      (3) Caution. The system flashes yellow. Caution alarms are normally advisory.

b. <u>Chart Objects</u>. Users can select specific chart objects (e.g., Aids to Navigation (ATON), Cautionary Areas, Land) and assign a specific alarm level based on distance to the object and other factors.

c. <u>Sensors</u>. The system can produce an alarm when a sensor fails, the connection is lost, or the data of the sensor is not valid.

d. <u>Targets</u>. Users can configure alarms for targets by changing the minimum Closest Point of Approach (CPA) distance or time. Setting both distance and time to a value of zero is considered disabling the target alarm.

7. <u>Display of Navigational Information</u>. Electronic navigation systems also permit the display of useful information for vessel navigation. Specific types of navigational information a system may display includes:

a. <u>Advance of Vessel Position</u>. Vessel position is advanced (direction and speed) between fixes based on the selected own vessel velocity vector. Several means of direction and speed may be available, depending on the positioning source in use and system capabilities. Ordered course and speed differs from course over ground and speed over ground or course and speed through the water.

b. <u>Dead Reckoning (DR)</u>. A properly maintained DR plot is the foundation for maintaining an acceptable estimate of the vessel's position between fixes, and it provides valuable information in evaluating the effects of external forces on the vessel and ensuring the safe navigation of the vessel.

c. <u>Set and Drift</u>. eNav systems have two ways to calculate set and drift. A thorough understanding of each method is essential to proper navigation, especially in restricted waters.

(1) <u>Computed</u>. Continuously updated set and drift obtained by comparing own ship heading to course over ground and own ship speed to speed over ground. This gives a constantly fluctuating "in the moment" set and drift.

(2) <u>Ordered</u>. Ordered course and speed are entered, set and drift is calculated over the entered fix interval, resulting in a long term set and drift, similar to paper chart calculations (i.e. instead of every second, set and drift is calculated every designated fix).

N. <u>Satellite Navigation Systems</u>. There are multiple Global Navigation Satellite Positioning Systems (GNSS) available, which enable precise navigation around the world. Coast Guard assets are required to use the United States Government owned and controlled Global Positioning System (GPS) for primary navigation and automated plotting mode. GPS positions can also be used for navigating in manual plotting mode. Alternate satellite positioning or terrestrial based triangulation systems, can be used to verify a vessel's position when navigating using traditional methods and manual plotting.

1. <u>GPS Corrections</u>. National Differential GPS (NDGPS) system and the Wide Area Augmentation System (WAAS) are the only GPS corrections currently authorized for Coast Guard vessel use in restricted waters (e.g., major ports). The Coast Guard began to reduce this service in 2018 and is scheduled to discontinue the entire NDGPS service from its remaining broadcast sites by the end of 2020.

2. <u>GPS Receiver and WAAS</u>. Units equipped with a GPS receiver capable of receiving GPS corrections from the WAAS are authorized to use this feature. WAAS is a satellite-based GPS augmentation system implemented by the Federal Aviation Administration to support lateral and vertical navigation for all phases of flight in the U.S.

3. <u>Deliberate GPS Disruptions</u>. The signals from all satellite positioning systems are limited in power and are very susceptible to jamming or spoofing. The operating bands for most satellite systems are close enough to one another that if one is being blocked or altered, others will likely be affected. Reporting procedures for GPS disruptions are found in Enclosure (8).

   a. Jamming is when a satellite positioning system's signal is blocked and a precise position is unable to be obtained.

   b. Spoofing is when a satellite positioning system's signal is altered with the objective of changing the targeted vessel's satellite position readout to a location other than where the vessel actually resides.

CHAPTER 3.   CUTTER NAVIGATION REQUIREMENTS

A. <u>Introduction</u>. COs/OICs must describe in their Command Navigation Standards how they will meet the requirements of this Chapter, accounting for the risks associated with their AOR(s) and mission set. See Chapter 2, Navigation Fundamentals, for general descriptions.

B. <u>Voyage Planning Requirements</u>. CO/OICs must ensure completion of the following items as part of the voyage planning process.

1. <u>Navigational Information</u>. The Command Navigation Standards must specify the following required navigational information to meet voyage planning requirements.

Cutter Navigational Information	
1. Navigational Draft.	11. Location of GPS antenna.
2. Safety Contour.	12. Distance from hawsepipe to alidade.*
3. Shallow Contour.	13. Distance from hawsepipe to GPS antenna.*
4. Safety Depth.	14. Distance from hawsepipe to stern.*
5. Length Overall.	15. Distance from radar antenna to hawsepipe.*
6. Vessel Beam.	16. Distance from GPS antenna to stern.*
7. Masthead height (fixed and unfixed, if applicable.)	17. Distance from radar antenna to stern.*
8. Unclassified tactical data.	18. Line handling commands. See Enclosure (5).
9. Full load draft.	19. Standard Helm commands. See Enclosure (6).
10. Height of bridge above the waterline.	20. Engine order commands vary between cutter classes based on engine configuration and equipment. COs/OICs must ensure Command Navigation Standards include standard engine order commands and engine/propulsion configurations as appropriate for the cutter.
(*Note – If applicable.)	

Table 3-1: Cutter Navigational Information

2. <u>Define Navigational Zones/Areas</u>. Command Navigation Standards must define applicable navigational zones/areas, which reflect the risk associated with locations within a unit's normal AOR. The following are zones/areas normally associated with cutters (as applicable, for AOR):

a. Shoal Water.

    b. Restricted Waters.

    c. Piloting Waters.

    d. Coastal Waters.

    e. Open Ocean.

3. Identify Appropriate Fix Interval. Fix intervals must be identified in the Command Navigation Standards for each navigational zone/area. Intervals must not exceed one hour without CO/OIC authorization. Regardless of navigation mode in use, fixing a cutter's position at regular intervals, coupled with an assessment of the cutter's navigation and maneuvering situation (e.g., speed of the vessel, proximity of shoal water, weather conditions, and mission parameters), helps ensure the safe navigation of the vessel.

4. Route Planning. Command Navigation Standards must provide guidance for route planning using electronic systems and must include, at a minimum:

    a. Timely identification and impact of Notice to Mariner/Local Notice to Mariner (NTM/LMN) issued since the last electronic chart update.

    b. CO/OIC approved tracklines, principal navigation routes, and waypoints.

    c. Maximum allowable cross track error along each route and/or track leg as appropriate.

5. Additional Navigational Requirements. Command Navigation Standards must provide guidance on the below Sections at a minimum:

    a. Unique Operations. Include specific requirements for special or AOR specific operations, such as high speed, pursuit, and/or aids to navigation.

    b. Speed Management Expectations. Rule six of the COLREGS/Inland Navigation Rules defines safe speed for all vessels. Units must include speed management expectations in their Command Navigation Standards. The intention is to make crews aware of the effects of excessive speed and over confidence aboard increasingly capable assets. In addition to the safe speed considerations discussed in COLREGS/Inland Navigation Rules, Command Navigation Standards must discuss unit/AOR specific considerations such as; operational urgency, local regulations, bridge resource management, and asset characteristics.

    c. Cell Phone and Mobile Electronics Usage. Define policy for the use of cell phones/ texting/mobile devices and phone/device applications on the bridge by watchstanders.

6. Chart and Publication Preparations. Charts (electronic and paper, as appropriate) must be currently corrected to ensure proper display and highlighting of hazards to navigation (e.g., overhead obstructions, prohibited areas, shoal water, etc.) along the intended route and within the AOR. On all charts used for navigation, crews must verify information is identical on each chart to ensure navigation decision-makers have the same navigational information/picture.

a. <u>General Chart and Publication Preparation Requirements</u>.

   (1) Conduct annual review of chart and publication holdings, and route any requests for new products or allowance changes via the chain of command.

   (2) Maintain an updated electronic chart portfolio.

   (3) Prior to getting underway, ensure all ready charts and any additional patrol specific charts and required publications (Coast Pilot, Light List, Tide Tables, and COLREGS/ Inland Navigation Rules) necessary for safe navigation are currently corrected and onboard (electronic or paper).

b. <u>Electronic Chart Preparations</u>.

   (1) If the eNav system permits, all tracklines on electronic charts used in restricted waters must display the following labels:

      (a) True Course.

      (b) Magnetic Course.

   (2) The Navigator must consult electronic chart and information products applicable to the intended route or AOR to ensure all available updates and precautions for the route or area are accounted for.

   (3) The eNav system (SINS-I, SINS-II, Seawatch, etc.) must make use of the depth contours function to highlight shoal water or a more conservative safety depth contour.

c. <u>Paper Chart Preparations (if utilized)</u>.

   (1) Designate a list of ready charts based on individual unit requirements. Any paper charts used for restricted waters navigation must be corrected prior to use and prepared in accordance with this Section's requirements. Paper charts used for restricted waters navigation must be signed, or otherwise certified, by the unit CO/OIC as being fully prepared, corrected, and ready for use.

   (2) Shoal Water must be penned in a color and weight that will stand out, even under night lighting.

   (3) Label CO/OIC approved tracklines on ready charts for restricted waters transits with the following:

      (a) True Course (only required for vessels fitted with a gyrocompass).

      (b) Magnetic Course.

      (c) Distance of each track leg.

(d) Intended Track Speed.

(e) Visual and radar navigation points. See Enclosure (7). Also listed in a gazetteer in accordance with Enclosure (9).

(f) Danger bearings/ranges to navigational hazards not marked by navigation aids.

(g) Turn bearings/ranges.

(h) Slide lines for advance and transfer based on the ship's tactical data for the intended speed/rudder combination.

(i) Label chart shifts on all charts. Bridge and CIC (if applicable) must shift charts within 1 fix interval and must avoid shifting paper charts at the same time or immediately prior to a turn.

(4) When plotting tracklines on paper charts for use outside of restricted waters, label with the following:

(a) True Course (only required for vessels fitted with a gyrocompass).

(b) Magnetic Course.

(c) Distance of Track Leg.

7. <u>Navigation Briefs</u>. Briefs are a critical element of the navigational planning process and ensure safe navigation of Coast Guard cutters. They are tailored specifically to operations and serve to ensure all members involved have a common understanding of the risks present and actions to mitigate those risks. Briefs must be conducted prior to getting underway, entering port and, if possible, prior to entering restricted waters and include the following, when applicable:

Cutter Navigation Brief Items	
1. Assignment of Navigation Team positions and review of duties as outlined in Enclosure (4).	18. Review of pertinent information from Fleet Guide, Coast Pilot, and Sailing Directions.
2. Review of charts and intended track including results of scanned route.	19. Expected sightings and characteristics of key aids to navigation.
3. Electronic chart selection, specific type (e.g., ENC, DNC, etc.) and paper chart selection (if used), and any known chart offset.	20. ATON discrepancies along track or other items of note from LNM, NTM, or current Broadcast Notice to Mariners.
4. Restricted, prohibited, and cautionary areas along intended track.	21. Anticipated vessel traffic (cutters should plan to avoid meeting deep draft vessels at turns or intersections).
5. Maximum allowable deviation from track and confirmation that electronic chart cross track warnings are aligned with max deviation from track, if applicable.	22. Environmental considerations including tides, currents, weather, and environmentally sensitive areas (e.g., marine sanctuaries). Note: Tide and current data should be available at all conning stations and CIC.
6. Planned speed of advance and maximum safe speed.	23. Areas where the cutter can/cannot anchor in an emergency.
7. Intended speed/rudder combination for turns, if different than specified standards.	24. Port or Vessel Traffic Service (VTS) requirements including speed limits, pilotage, working frequencies, and check in points.
8. Chart shifts, if paper charts are used.	25. Agreed-upon rendezvous/recovery points.
9. Demarcation line crossings.	26. Traffic Separation Schemes.
10. Planned fix interval.	27. Engineering plant status.
11. AIS mode to be used (e.g., normal, receive only, encrypted, etc.). Method and date of most recent AIS vessel information verification for cutters and cutter boats. Ensure encrypted AIS key is current per Chapter 5 D.6 of Reference (l).	28. Identification of hazards to navigation and how the risks will be mitigated and/or accepted, including: Navigation warnings, danger bearings/ranges, danger soundings, bridge vertical clearances, proximity-guard alarms, depth alarms, etc.
12. Navigation equipment status.	29. Mooring or anchoring arrangements including time to moor/unmoor and pier face.
13. eNav back up arrangement, if applicable.	30. Port information and availability of shore-based resources (if applicable).
14. Status of electronic position fixing systems (GPS/NDGPS) to include expected accuracy and outages.	31. Anticipated time of setting the Special Sea Detail, Anchoring and Mooring Bills, Engineering Restricted Maneuvering Doctrine, and Navigation Detail.
15. International Association of Marine Aids to Navigation and Lighthouse Authorities (IALA) buoyage system and whether inbound or outbound.	32. Conduct risk assessment in accordance with Reference (g).
16. Communication requirements.	33. Conduct debriefs following navigation evolutions to evaluate and recognize performance.
17. Chart datum (e.g., WGS 84) and verification of positioning source datum.	34. The planned mode of operation (DP, harbor, cruise) for the transit.

Table 3-2: Cutter Navigation Brief Items

8. <u>Verify Essential Systems are Ready for Navigation</u>.

   a. Prior to getting underway or entering restricted waters, conduct a steering test and propulsion check in accordance with Reference (a).

   b. Prior to getting underway, verify the accuracy of all positioning sources and navigational equipment (e.g., GPS, radar, gyrocompass/alternate heading source, etc.).

9. <u>Set Appropriate Navigation Station Manning Levels</u>. (e.g., Special Sea Detail)

10. <u>Select and Prepare for Appropriate Navigation Mode</u>. See Table 3-3 below:

Navigation Mode	Chart Requirements	System Requirements	Other Requirements
Automated Plotting	(1) Updated electronic chart in use in accordance with approved chart hierarchy.	(1) Fully mission capable eNav system properly configured IAW Command Navigation Standards.	(1) Unit capable of transitioning to an approved redundant or back-up system in the event of a component or system failure **_or_** use manual plotting methods until system restored.
Manual Plotting	(1) Updated electronic and/or current edition of paper chart is onboard. (2) Corrected paper chart is required if planned to be used as a primary means of navigation. (3) Corrected paper chart is not required for restricted waters navigation if used only as a temporary response to an eNav failure.	(1) Operable electronic system available that is capable of recording and plotting lines of position and ranges to provide fix information. Otherwise, paper chart navigation using traditional navigation methods is required. (2) Radar and visual bearing objects are labeled and displayed in the eNav system for restricted water transits.	(1) Unit proficiency in traditional navigation methods, including the use of seaman's eye.

Table 3-3: Cutter Navigation Mode Requirements

2. <u>Enable Appropriate Sensor and System Alarms (if equipped)</u>.

   a. Depth Alarm (properly configured for transducer offset and set to activate at depth equal-to or more-than Navigational Draft, as per Maintenance Procedures Cards (MPC)).

   b. Maximum allowable Cross Track Error.

C. <u>Voyage Monitoring Requirements</u>.

1. <u>Fix Vessel Position</u>. At the fix intervals prescribed in the Command Navigation Standards, determine the vessel's position using visual and/or electronic means. Record the fix and label it

with the time and proper symbol, consistent with the navigation mode in use and capability of the eNav system (if applicable). Enclosure (7) contains standard navigation plotting symbols.

2. <u>Verify Vessel Position</u>. To avoid over-reliance on a single source of information, verify vessel position at each fix using all means available.

   a. Use a secondary means to verify vessel position. Techniques include soundings, visual observations, danger ranges/bearings, set and drift, radar overlay and chart matching, and positive identification and relative position of aids to navigation and other charted features or landmarks.

   b. Do not erase or delete fixes because they appear in error.

   c. If position ambiguity exists, all appropriate team members (e.g., OOD, Conning Officer, Coxswain) must be verbally informed and another fix taken immediately to ascertain the vessel's position.

3. <u>Evaluate Position Fixes</u>. At each prescribed fix interval, members responsible for the safe navigation of cutters and boats must ensure evaluation of the vessel's position with due regard to, at a minimum, the proximity of shoal water, environmental conditions, and mission parameters.

4. <u>Set and Drift</u>. Command navigation standards must specify that a computation of set and drift is reported at specific fix intervals for the waters in which the cutter is operating.

5. <u>Take Appropriate Precautions</u>. If at any time fix quality comes into question, particularly while operating in restricted waters (e.g., near shoal water or obstructions), crews must initiate appropriate actions to minimize risk to the vessel and crew in accordance with the Command Navigation Standards. Some actions may include:

   a. Reducing speed.

   b. Taking all way off.

   c. Increasing fix frequency.

6. <u>GPS Accuracy and Outage Reporting</u>.

   a. <u>GPS Accuracy</u>. Command Navigation Standards must define times and intervals for verifying GPS equipment accuracy to ensure safe navigation (e.g., before getting underway and entering restricted waters, daily for cutters operating in rivers or harbors, daily for boats, etc.). Units should not normally use another GPS unit to determine the accuracy and proper operation of the primary GPS unit.

   b. <u>Outage Reporting</u>. All Coast Guard GPS/NDGPS/WAAS users must report GPS outages, anomalies, and suspected spoofing or jamming. Enclosure (8) provides detailed information concerning reporting processes. Units operating in areas where deliberate GPS disruptions can be expected will normally receive a pre-deployment brief on these GPS disruptions.

D. Electronic Navigation Requirements.

1. Restricting Applications. On computers designated specifically for navigation or situational awareness, only navigation related applications must be open. The navigation software must be the active application and operators must only minimize it when using another navigation-related application (e.g., Total Tides, System to Estimate Latitude and Longitude Astronomically (STELLA)). Unauthorized applications not part of the system baseline must not be installed.

2. Personal Navigation Applications. The use of personal navigation applications using cellular/GPS technology is not permitted for Coast Guard navigation.

3. Electronic Navigation as Primary Means of Navigation. The use of Coast Guard installed electronic navigation systems is approved as the primary means of navigation aboard Coast Guard cutters. Additionally, personnel must understand how to load/install charts on electronic navigation systems in order to use them as a primary means of navigation. Table 3-3 displays the basic requirements to use either the automated plotting or manual plotting mode as the primary means of navigation.

4. eNav Display. The Command Navigation Standards must include guidance for eNav display parameters necessary to ensure safe navigation for all cutters under their command in the following categories. (See Chapter 2, Navigation Fundamentals for definitions):

   a. Display Base. (Depth displayed should be actual water depth, not depth beneath keel/transducer.)

   b. Standard Display.

   c. All Other Information.

5. Advance of Vessel Position. When available in the eNav system, the input for own vessel direction and speed must be in accordance with the Command Navigation Standards and standard system documentation.

6. Dead Reckoning (DR). When DR features are available in the eNav system, they must be used, and their use must be defined in the Command Navigation Standards.

7. System Configuration and Settings. The Command Navigation Standards must detail system configuration and settings for each:

   a. Navigation zone/area.

   b. Navigation evolution requiring unique configuration (e.g., anchoring).

   c. Navigation mode.

8. Profiles. CO/OICs must include appropriate profile information in the Command Navigation Standards for specific Navigational Zones/Areas. The proper use of filters will facilitate safe navigation for cutters and boats under their command.

9. <u>Alarms</u>. The Command Navigation Standards must identify alarm settings for each Navigation Zone/Area (e.g., depth alarms, transducer offsets, cross track distance).

10. <u>Approved Electronic Chart Hierarchy</u>. Based on data accuracy, CO/OICs must follow the electronic chart type hierarchy in Table 2-2 to the maximum extent possible. CO/OICs have discretion to authorize situational variances (due to chart quality, etc.), provided such variances are briefed to the command and the navigation team (normally at the navigation brief) prior to deviation. However, if any standing deviations from Table 2-2 exist for a particular unit, the Command Navigation Standards must document them.

11. <u>Currently Corrected Electronic Chart Data</u>. To be used for navigation, charts must be currently corrected.

    a. An electronic chart is considered currently corrected if it has been updated within the last 45 days. However, it is recommend to download the latest chart updates at every opportunity.

    b. Full file replacement of the electronic chart data is the recommended method to update electronic charts (e.g., cell, library, chart, or chartlet). When available, full file replacement should be the normal method of updating charts. NGA's website provides DNC full file replacement charts. This is the only approved method of updating DNC charts.

    c. Users can enter manual corrections into the eNav system when connectivity or mail delivery prevents crews from obtaining full file replacements. Cutters should use this method on a limited basis. The following are approved sources for manual corrections:

        (1) The cognizant hydrographic office (e.g., NOAA, USACE, NGA, Canadian Hydrographic Services (CHS), United Kingdom Hydrographic Office (UKHO) etc.)

        (2) LNM

        (3) NTM

12. <u>Display Matching</u>. When the system displays radar and electronic chart data on the same screen, the display must match in scale, orientation, and projection.

13. <u>Discrepancies</u>.

    a. Report chart display discrepancies and discrepancies in chart data to the Coast Guard Navigation Center via priority message to COGARD NAVCEN ALEXANDRIA VA//NIS//.

    b. For ATON chart discrepancies, notify the appropriate CG District Waterways (dpw) office via priority message traffic, with COGARD NAVCEN ALEXANDRIA VA//NIS// and COMDT COGARD WASHINGTON DC//CG-NAV// as information addressees. In all cases, reporting units must provide an ENC Cell Name and a detailed description of error(s). Local Sector/ATON units should also be notified.

E. Paper Chart Navigation Requirements.

1. Charts. When required by Table 3-3, use only currently corrected charts produced by an approved IHO, giving priority to NOAA and NGA charts. NAVCEN is the paper chart account and portfolio manager. The primary source for paper charts is the Defense Logistics Agency.

   a. Paper charts are currently corrected if they are both the most current edition and corrected up to the latest LNM and NTM.

   b. For units underway and not able to receive the most current edition or the latest LNM and NTM, paper charts are still considered currently corrected until returning to port.

2. Print on Demand Charts. Print on Demand (POD) charts, if used, must be maintained by applying LNM and NTM corrections subsequent to dates listed on the POD chart. Coast Guard units are not authorized to produce their own POD charts for navigation. Raster based POD Charts may be procured from third party commercial providers which have been certified by NOAA/NGA. NOAA is currently working to develop standard formatting rules under which Print on Demand Charts derived from ENC data will meet safety of navigation requirements. Until such time as ENC Paper Chart Policy has been more fully developed, POD charts derived from ENC data are not approved for primary means of navigation and should be considered a situational awareness tool.

3. Fixes. Command Navigation Standards must detail fix intervals when using paper charts as the primary means of navigation.

   a. The fix intervals must ensure safe navigation given the risks present for the navigation zone/area.

   b. When three LOPs are not simultaneously available, advance previous LOPs to a common time to create a running fix.

   c. Do not erase a fix because it appears to be in error. Rather, take another fix immediately to ascertain the vessel's position and the source of the error. Upon determining the source of the error, correct for the error so that it does not recur.

4. Set and Drift.

   a. If fix interval is three minutes or greater, determine set and drift with every fix.

   b. If the fix interval is less than three minutes, determine set and drift with every second fix.

   c. If there is no fix, consider set and drift as part of determining an estimated position (EP).

5. Dead Reckoning (DR). When plotting DRs, properly label and project the track for at least two fix intervals and utilize the six rules of DR (as described in Chapter 2, Navigation Fundamentals) to maintain the plot.

F. Cutter Boat Specific Navigation Requirements.

1. Navigational and Voyage Planning Information. The Command Navigation Standards must specify the following required navigational information for cutter boats to meet voyage planning requirements:

Cutter Boat Navigational and Voyage Planning Information	

a. Boat Characteristics:
 	
  (1) Length Overall
  (2) Beam
  (3) Operational Draft
  (4) Maximum and Fixed Height Above the Waterline
  (5) Trailer Weight
  (6) Distance between transducer and lowest point on the hull
  (7) Lowest point on the hull
	c. Environmental Limitations and Operating Parameters:
	
	  (1) Maximum Winds and Seas
	  (2) Maximum Operating Distance from the Cutter
	  (3) Maximum Crew Endurance
	  (4) Maximum Seas for Launch and Recovery
	  (5) Maximum Cruising Speed and engine RPMs

b. Crew Manning Requirements and Personnel Limits:
 	
  (1) Crew Requirements for Launch and Recovery
  (2) Maximum Personnel Limits
  (3) Crewing Requirements for law enforcement, pursuit, aids to navigation, and other operations.
	d. Other Navigation Requirements (as applicable):
	
	  (1) Define high speed operations.
	  (2) Include speed management expectations
	  (3) Include specific requirements for high speed, pursuit, aids to navigation, or other special operations to include authorized training areas, waiver processes, and crewing requirements

Table 3-4: Cutter Boat Navigational and Voyage Planning Information

2. Additional Voyage Planning Requirements.

  a. General. These requirements should be incorporated as applicable to installed equipment and to the maximum extent practical.

    (1) Ensure boat checks are completed within 24 hours of boat operations.

    (2) Using the boat specific operator's handbook, ensure equipment is functional and/or discrepancies have been identified and mitigation strategy discussed.

    (3) Fathometer set-up and use.

    (4) Required fix intervals.

(5) Navigation mode requirements.

(6) Approved electronic charting package setup to include cross track errors and waypoint pass criteria.

b. Route Planning. Identify command approved routes for local or AOR specific operations.

c. Define Navigational Zones/Areas. Command Navigation Standards must define applicable navigational zones/areas, which reflect the risk associated with locations within a unit's normal AOR. The following are the zones/areas normally associated with cutter boats (as applicable, based on AOR)

(1) Shoal Water.

(2) Restricted Waters.

(3) Coastal Waters.

(4) Open Ocean.

(5) Principle Navigation Routes, including special training areas.

(6) While in sight of cutter, electronic or visual, cutter can assume navigational picture for cutter boat in special circumstances. Due care must be exercised by the cutter to monitor changes in the cutter boat's navigational zone and proximity to navigational hazards.

d. Chart and Publication Preparations. When equipped, charts (electronic) must be currently corrected to ensure proper display and highlighting of hazards to navigation (e.g., overhead obstructions, prohibited areas, shoal water, etc.) along the intended route and within the AOR. The CO/OIC must approve tracklines and principal navigation routes for assigned cutter boats. Paper charts are not required to be maintained aboard.

(1) An electronic chart is considered currently corrected if it has been corrected within the last six months.

(2) The Coast Guard has contracted to provide updated electronic charts for SINS-II equipped cutter and cutter boats every six months. Cutters and cutter boats do not automatically receive updated electronic charts for SINS-I equipment. In the event that SINS electronic charts are out of date (longer than six months old) CO/OICs must specifically address and authorized use of SINS as primary means of navigation.

(3) The eNav system (SINS-I or SINS-II) must make use of the depth contours function to highlight shoal water or a more conservative safety depth contour. The use of this function can be waived in Command Navigation Standards for areas where the use of this function would prevent the effective use of the eNav system.

e. Boat Crew Briefs. Briefs are a critical element of the navigational planning process and ensure safe navigation of Coast Guard cutter boats. Cutter boat Coxswains are not required to complete an AOR familiarization. Therefore, briefs for cutter boats operating in restricted waters are more extensive than those required for shore-based boats. Cutter boat crew briefs are conducted prior to all cutter boat operations. Briefs must include the following information, when applicable:

Cutter Boat Crew Brief Items	
1. Conduct risk assessment in accordance with Reference (g).	5. Discussion of any pertinent environmental factors and considerations.
2. Discussion of planned boat crew assignments.	6. Equipment Status of Boat and cutter's boat handling equipment.
3. Review of the intended route (when operating out of sight of the cutter or in areas with navigation hazards or shoal water.	7. Personal Protective Equipment Requirements: Include mission specific needs, such as high speed, law enforcement, cold weather, and pursuit operations.
4. Review of any known hazards to navigation or shoal water and anticipated vessel traffic.	8. Communications Plan and Schedule

Table 3-5: Cutter Boat Crew Brief Items

3. <u>Seaman's Eye</u>. For cutter boats not equipped with standard Coast Guard electronic navigation systems or operating in sight of the cutter, seaman's eye can be the primary means of navigation. If a cutter boat does not have an installed Coast Guard electronic navigation system and must operate outside the cutter's line of sight, the transit must be conducted in definitive navigation channels with sufficient aids to navigation and/or landmarks (i.e. buoys, structures, river banks, ranges, enclosed sections of the Intra-Coastal Waterway (ICW) etc.) to ensure its safe navigation. Fixes are not required while using seaman's eye.

4. <u>Electronic Navigation Requirements/Restricting Applications</u>. Within SINS, only navigation related applications must be open. Unauthorized applications not part of the system baseline must not be installed.

5. <u>Cell Phone and Mobile Electronics Usage</u>.

   a. In accordance with Reference (c), the use of cell phones/texting/mobile devices and phone/device applications aboard boats is prohibited without permission of the Coxswain; permission can be granted only on a case by case basis.

   b. In the case where the use of a cellphone/texting device is approved, the Coxswain must assure a safe and efficient navigational environment by posting proper lookouts and the assigned navigation support functions are attentive to their duties.

   (1) Helmsman is prohibited from using a cell phone/texting device.

6. <u>Personal Navigation Applications</u>. The use of personal navigation applications using cellular/GPS technology are not permitted for Coast Guard boat navigation.

CHAPTER 4.   **SHORE–BASED BOAT NAVIGATION REQUIREMENTS**

A. Introduction. COs/OICs must describe in their Command Navigation Standards how they will meet the requirements of this Chapter, accounting for the risks associated with their AOR(s) and mission set. See Chapter 2, Navigation Fundamentals, for general descriptions.

B. Voyage Planning Requirements. CO/OICs must ensure completion of the following items as part of the voyage planning process.

1. Navigational Information. The Command Navigation Standards must specify the following required navigational information to meet voyage planning requirements.

   a. Navigational Draft.

   b. Fixed and unfixed height.

2. Define Navigational Zones/Areas. Command Navigation Standards must define applicable navigational zones/areas, which reflect the risk associated with locations within a unit's normal AOR. The following are the zones/areas normally associated with boats (as applicable, based on AOR):

   a. Shoal Water.

   b. Restricted Waters.

   c. Coastal Waters.

   d. Open Ocean.

   e. Approved Navigation Routes.

   f. AOR Key Waypoints.

   g. AOR Key Areas.

3. Identify Appropriate Fix Interval. Fix intervals are identified for each navigational zone/area based on risk. Intervals must not exceed one hour without CO/OIC authorization. Regardless of navigation mode in use, this interval structures the recurring assessment of the vessel's navigation and maneuvering situation (e.g., speed of the vessel, proximity of shoal water, weather conditions, and mission parameters) to ensure the safe navigation of the vessel. Include required fix intervals in the Command Navigation Standards.

4. Route Planning. Command Navigation Standards must provide guidance for eNav route planning and must include, at a minimum:

   a. Timely identification and impact of Notice to Mariner/Local Notice to Mariner (NTM/LMN) issued since electronic chart data update.

   b. CO/OIC approved track lines and waypoints.

    c. Maximum allowable cross track error along each route and/or track leg as appropriate.

5. <u>Additional Navigational Requirements</u>.

    a. <u>Unique Operations</u>. Include specific requirements for high speed, pursuit, aids to navigation, or other special operations to include authorized training areas, waiver processes, and crewing requirements (as applicable).

    b. <u>Speed Management Expectations</u>. Rule six of the COLREGS/Inland Navigation Rules defines safe speed for all vessels. Units must include speed management expectations in their Command Navigation Standards. The intention is to make crews aware of the effects of excessive speed and over confidence aboard increasingly capable boats. In addition to the safe speed considerations discussed in COLREGS/Inland Navigation Rules, Command Navigation Standards must discuss unit/AOR specific considerations such as; operational urgency, local regulations, crew cabin management, and asset characteristics.

    c. <u>Cell Phone and Mobile Electronics Usage</u>.

        (1) In accordance with Reference (c), the use of cell phones/texting/mobile devices and phone/device applications aboard Boat Forces assets is prohibited without permission of the Coxswain; permission can be granted only on a case by case basis.

        (2) In the case where the use of a cellphone/texting device is approved, the Coxswain must assure a safe and efficient navigational environment by posting proper lookouts and the assigned navigation support functions are attentive to their duties.

        (3) Helmsman is prohibited from using a cell phone/texting device.

6. <u>Chart and Publication Preparations</u>. Charts (electronic and paper, as appropriate) must be currently corrected to ensure proper display and highlighting of hazards to navigation (e.g., overhead obstructions, prohibited areas, shoal water, etc.) along the intended route and within the AOR.

    a. <u>General Chart and Publication Preparation Requirements</u>. Required publications are onboard (electronic or paper) as per Enclosure (13).

    b. <u>Electronic Chart Preparations</u>.

        (1) If the eNav system permits, all tracklines on electronic charts must display Magnetic Course.

        (2) The boat crew must consult electronic chart and information products applicable to the intended route or AOR to ensure all available updates and precautions for the route or AOR are accounted for.

        (3) The eNav system (SINS-I or SINS-II) must make use of the depth contours function to highlight shoal water or a more conservative safety depth contour. The use of this

function can be waived in Command Navigation Standards for boats where the use of this function would prevent the effective use of the eNav system.

   c. <u>Paper Chart Preparations</u>.

      (1) Maintain a portfolio of currently corrected master paper charts onboard the unit.

      (2) Shoal Water must be penned in a color and weight that will stand out, even under night lighting.

      (3) Label CO/OIC approved tracklines on unit master paper charts with the following.

         (a) Magnetic Course.

         (b) Distance of each track leg.

         (c) Radar navigation points (restricted waters only). See Enclosure (7).

7. <u>Boat Crew Briefs</u>. Briefs are a critical element of the navigational planning process and ensure safe navigation of Coast Guard boats. They are tailored specifically to operations and serve to ensure all members involved have a common understanding of the risks present and actions to mitigate those risks. Per Reference (c), Area of Responsibility (AOR) familiarization ensures boat crews are well versed in local navigation requirements. Boat crew briefs are conducted prior to getting underway and, if possible, prior to entering restricted waters. Briefs must include the following information, when applicable:

Boat Crew Brief Items	
1. Review of Voyage Plan	6. Environmental considerations including tides, currents, weather (e.g., winds, precipitation, visibility), and environmentally sensitive sea areas (e.g., marine sanctuaries).
2. Assignment of crew positions.	7. AIS mode to be used (e.g., normal, receive only, encrypted, etc.). Method and date of most recent AIS vessel information verification for boats. Ensure encrypted AIS key is current per Chapter 5 D.6 of Reference (l).
3. Safe speed for mission and conditions.	8. Conduct risk assessments in accordance with Reference (g).
4. Identification of hazards to navigation.	9. Conduct a post-operations debrief to evaluate and recognize performance.
5. Anticipated vessel traffic.	

Table 4-1: Boat Crew Brief Items

8. <u>Verify Essential Systems are Ready for Navigation</u>.

    a. Daily and, if possible, prior to mooring, conduct a steering test and propulsion check.

    b. Daily, verify all positioning sources and navigational equipment for accuracy.

9. <u>Set Appropriate Watch Station Manning Levels</u> (e.g., assigning boat crew specific navigation support functions).

10. <u>Select and Prepare for the Appropriate Navigation Mode</u>. See Table 4-2 below:

Navigation Mode	Chart Requirements	System Requirements	Other Requirements
Automated Plotting	(1) Updated electronic chart in use in accordance with approved chart hierarchy.	(1) Fully mission capable eNav system properly configured IAW Command Navigation Standards.	(1) Unit capable of transitioning to an approved redundant or back-up system in the event of a component or system failure _**or**_ use manual plotting methods until system restored.
Manual Plotting	(1) Updated electronic and/or current edition of paper chart is onboard. (2) Corrected paper chart is required if planned to be used as a primary means of navigation. (3) Corrected paper chart is not required for restricted waters navigation if used only as a temporary response to an eNav failure.	(1) Operable electronic system available that is capable of recording and plotting lines of position and ranges to provide fix information. Otherwise, paper chart navigation using traditional navigation methods is required. (2) Radar and visual bearing objects are labeled and displayed in the eNav system for restricted water transits.	(1) Unit proficiency in traditional navigation methods, including the use of seaman's eye.

Table 4-2: Boat Navigation Mode Requirements

11. <u>Enable Appropriate Sensor and System Alarms (if equipped)</u>.

    a. Depth Alarm (properly configured for transducer offset and set to activate at depth equal-to or more-than Navigational Draft, as per Maintenance Procedures Cards (MPC)).

    b. Maximum allowable Cross Track Error.

C. <u>Voyage Monitoring Requirements</u>. The coxswain must continually monitor the boat's position and then verify and evaluate it with one or more of the following: seaman's eye navigation, soundings, danger ranges/bearings, set and drift, radar overlay and chart matching, and positive identification and relative position of aids to navigation and other charted features or landmarks to ensure the safe and prudent navigation of the boat. Coxswains must avoid an over-reliance on installed eNav system information or any other single source of navigation information. If position ambiguity exists, the boatcrew must use all available means to ascertain the boat's position.

1. <u>Procedures for eNav Failure.</u> Command Navigation Standards must specify procedures for navigating boats in the event of a complete eNav system package failure. This includes prescribed fix intervals and fix verification/evaluation procedures for their boats. In these rare situations, boat crews must be trained and proficient in traditional navigation methods along with seaman's eye to safely navigate the boat until the eNav package can be restored to a fully mission capable status.

2. <u>Take Appropriate Precautions</u>. If at any time fix quality comes into question, particularly while operating in high risk areas (e.g., near shoal water or obstructions), crews must initiate appropriate actions to minimize risk to the vessel and crew in accordance with the Command Navigation Standards. Some actions may include:

   a. Reducing speed.

   b. Taking all way off.

   c. Increasing fix frequency.

3. <u>GPS Accuracy and Outage Reporting.</u>

   a. <u>GPS Accuracy</u>. Command Navigation Standards must define times and intervals for verifying GPS equipment accuracy to ensure safe navigation (e.g., before getting underway and entering restricted waters, daily for cutters operating in rivers or harbors, daily for boats, etc.). Units should not normally use another GPS unit to determine the accuracy and proper operation of the primary GPS unit.

   b. <u>Outage Reporting</u>. All Coast Guard GPS/NDGPS/WAAS users must report GPS outages, anomalies, and suspected spoofing of jamming. Enclosure (8) provides detailed information concerning reporting processes. Units operating in areas where deliberate GPS disruptions are potentially expected should normally receive a pre-deployment brief.

D. <u>Electronic Navigation Requirements.</u>

1. <u>Restricting Applications</u>. On computers designated specifically for navigation or situational awareness (SINS), only navigation related applications must be open. Unauthorized applications not part of the system baseline must not be installed.

2. <u>Personal Navigation Applications</u>. The use of personal navigation applications using cellular/GPS technology are not permitted for Coast Guard boat navigation.

3. <u>eNav Display</u>. The Command Navigation Standards must include guidance for eNav display parameters necessary to ensure safe navigation for all boats under their command in the following categories. (See Chapter 2, Navigation Fundamentals for definitions)

   a. Display Base.

    b. Standard Display.

    c. All Other Information.

4. Profiles. CO/OICs must include appropriate profile information in the Command Navigation Standards for specific Navigational Zones/Area to facilitate safe navigation for boats under their command (if applicable).

5. Alarms. The Command Navigation Standards must identify alarm settings for each Navigation Zone/Area (e.g., depth alarms, transducer offsets, cross track distance).

6. Approved Electronic Chart Hierarchy. Based on data accuracy, CO/OICs must follow the electronic chart type hierarchy in Table 2-2 to the maximum possible extent. CO/OICs have discretion to authorize situational variances (due to chart quality, etc.), provided such variances are briefed to the command and the navigation team (normally at the navigation brief) prior to deviation. However, if any standing deviations from Table 2-2 exist for a particular unit, the Command Navigation Standards must document them.

7. Currently Corrected Electronic Chart Data. To be used for navigation, charts must be corrected with the latest Notice to Mariners and Local Notices to Mariners.

    a. An electronic chart is considered currently corrected if it has been corrected within the last six months.

    b. The Coast Guard has contracted to provide updated electronic charts for SINS equipped boats every six months. In the event that SINS electronic charts are out of date (longer than six months old) CO/OICs may authorize use of SINS as primary means of navigation if a currently corrected paper chart is onboard.

8. Discrepancies.

    a. Report chart display discrepancies and discrepancies in chart data to the Coast Guard Navigation Center via priority message to COGARD NAVCEN ALEXANDRIA VA//NIS//.

    b. For ATON chart discrepancies, notify the appropriate CG District Waterways (dpw) office via priority message traffic, with COGARD NAVCEN ALEXANDRIA VA//NIS// and COMDT COGARD WASHINGTON DC//CG-NAV// as information addressees. In all cases, reporting units must provide an ENC Cell Name and a detailed description of error(s). Local Sector/ATON units should also be notified.

E. Paper Chart Navigation Requirements.

1. Charts. When required by Table 4-2, use only currently corrected charts produced by an approved IHO, giving priority to NOAA and NGA charts. Paper charts are currently corrected if they are both the most current edition and corrected up to the latest LNM and NTM. NAVCEN is the paper chart account and portfolio manager. The primary source for paper charts is the Defense Logistics Agency.

2. <u>Print on Demand Charts</u>. Print on Demand (POD) charts, if used, must be maintained by applying LNM and NTM corrections subsequent to dates listed on the POD chart. Coast Guard units are not authorized to produce their own POD charts for navigation. Raster based POD Charts may be procured from third party commercial providers which have been certified by NOAA/NGA. NOAA is currently working to develop standard formatting rules under which Print on Demand Charts derived from ENC data will meet safety of navigation requirements. Until such time as ENC Paper Chart Policy has been more fully developed, POD charts derived from ENC data are not approved for primary means of navigation and should be considered a situational awareness tool.

3. <u>Fixes</u>. Command Navigation Standards must detail fix intervals when using paper charts as the primary means of navigation.

   a. The fix intervals must ensure safe navigation given the risks present for the navigation zone/area.

   b. Do not erase a fix because it appears to be in error. Rather, take another fix immediately to ascertain the vessel's position and the source of the error. Upon determining the source of the error, correct for the error so that it does not recur.

4. <u>Set and Drift</u>.

   a. If fix interval is three minutes or greater, determine set and drift with every fix.

   b. If the fix interval is less than three minutes, determine set and drift with every second fix.

   c. If there is no fix, consider set and drift as part of determining an estimated position (EP).

5. <u>Dead Reckoning (DR)</u>. When plotting DRs, properly label and project the track for at least two fix intervals and utilize the Six rules of DR (as described in Chapter 2, Navigation Fundamentals) to maintain the plot.

CHAPTER 5.   COMMAND NAVIGATION STANDARDS CONTENT REQUIREMENTS

A. <u>General</u>. The Command Navigation Standards must integrate official guidance and unit-specific requirements into a cohesive unit Instruction that details navigational practices for a particular unit.

B. <u>Command Navigation Standards Content Requirements</u>. The Command Navigation Standards must address the items below:

Command Navigation Standards Content Requirement	Chapter References		
	Cutters	**Cutter Boats**	**Boats**
1. Identify Command Navigation Standards Familiarization Requirements			
a. Specify personnel required to review	Required, but no Chapter reference		
b. Identify review frequencies and method for documenting review	Required, but no Chapter reference		
2. Identify Voyage Planning Requirements			
a. Identify navigational information	3.B.1	3.F.1	4.B.1
b. Define navigational zones/areas	3.B.2	3.F.2.c	4.B.2
c. Identify fix interval	3.B.3	3.F.2.a.(4)	4.B.3
d. Provide guidance for route planning	3.B.4	3.F.2.b	4.B.4
e. Additional Navigational Requirements	3.B.5	3.F.1	4.B.5
f. Identify required chart and publication preparations	3.B.6	3.F.2.d	4.B.6
(1) General	3.B.6.a	Not required	4.B.6.a
(2) Electronic	3.B.6.b	3.F.2.d	4.B.6.b
(3) Paper	3.B.6.c	Not required	4.B.6.c
g. Identify required brief items	3.B.7	3.F.3	4.B.7
h. Specify how to verify essential systems are ready for navigation	3.B.8	3.F.2.a	4.B.8
i. Specify how to set appropriate watch station manning levels	3.B.9 & Encl. (4)	3.F.1.b	4.B.9
j. Specify how to select and prepare for appropriate navigation mode	3.B.10	3.F.2.a.(5)	4.B.10
k. Specify how to enable appropriate sensors and systems alarms (if equipped)	3.B.11	3.F.2.a.(6)	4.B.11
3. Identify Voyage Monitoring Requirements			
a. Specify how to Fix Vessel Position	3.C.1	N/A	4.C

b. Specify how to Verify Vessel Position	3.C.2	N/A	4.C
c. Specify how to Evaluate Vessel Position	3.C.3	Not required	4.C
d. Specify requirements for Set and Drift	3.C.4	Not required	N/A
e. Specify Precautionary Actions	3.C.5	Not required	4.C.2
f. Specify GPS usage information	3.C.6	Not required	4.C.3
4. Identify Electronic Navigation Requirements			
a. Identify eNav Display requirements	3.D.4	Not required	4.D.2
b. Identify Advance of Vessel Position requirements	3.D.5	Not required	N/A
c. Identify Dead Reckoning usage	3.D.6	Not required	N/A
d. Identify Systems Configurations and Settings	3.D.7	Not required	N/A
e. Identify Profiles information	3.D.8	Not required	4.D.3
f. Identify Alarms Settings	3.D.9	Not required	4.D.4
g. Identify Electronic Chart Hierarchy	3.D.10	Not required	4.D.5
h. Identify requirements for Currently Corrected Electronic Chart Data	3.D.11	Not required	4.D.6
i. Identify requirements for Display Matching	3.D.12	Not required	Not required
5. Identify Paper Chart Navigation Requirements			
a. Identify Paper Chart requirements	3.E.1	Not required	4.E.1
b. Identify Fix Intervals	3.E.3	Not required	4.E.3
c. Identify Set and Drift requirements	3.E.4	Not required	4.E.4
d. Identify Dead Reckoning requirements	3.E.5	Not required	4.E.5
6. Identify Navigation Log/Checklists Requirements			
a. Identify Navigation Log/Checklist Requirements	Encl. (2) & (9), Ref. (J)	Not required	Not required

Table 5-1: Command Navigation Standards Content Requirements

CHAPTER 6.   **COMPLETELY PAPERLESS CHART NAVIGATION**

A. <u>Background/Commercial Chart Carriage Requirements</u>. All commercial ships greater than 500GT that must comply with the 1974 International Convention for the Safety of Life at Sea (SOLAS) are required by the International Maritime Organization (IMO) to use ENCs within an Electronic Chart Display and Information System (ECDIS). If they have a second independent ECDIS, they are not required to have any paper charts aboard. The USCG Navigation and Vessel Inspection Circular 01-16 CH 1 allows U.S. flagged commercial vessels engaged in domestic voyages to use and carry electronic ENC format charts as equivalent to raster format paper chants. When utilizing this equivalency, commercial mariners are not required to separately use and maintain paper charts for primary navigation means.

B. <u>Sun-setting of Raster/Paper Charts</u>. The National Oceanic and Atmospheric Administration (NOAA) stopped printing paper charts in 2013. As part of their 2017 - National Charting Plan, NOAA is preparing to stop issuing updates to their raster charts. NOAA will focus efforts on continuously updating ENC data sets available for both electronic (automated) and manual (paper) navigation. Efforts are currently underway to develop a standardized print on demand paper chart schema utilizing the ENC data. NOAA will continue to certify third party commercial providers which are capable of producing high quality paper charts using the ENC data. The 2016 revision to the Coast Guard Navigation Standards allowed units to no longer continuously update paper charts, with the exception of command designated ready charts, when holding the current edition of required paper charts aboard.

C. <u>Authorized Paperless Coast Guard Vessels</u>. The list of cutters and boats linked below are authorized for completely paperless navigation based on system redundancy, proficiency, and readiness to solely navigate using their installed eNav systems. These units are not required to carry paper charts aboard unless electronic charts are unavailable in an area they are operating. If operating in areas where approved electronic charts are unavailable, units must maintain proficiency with manual plotting on paper charts. This list will be updated and maintained at:
https://cg.portal.uscg.mil/units/cg751/NAV/Forms/AllItems.aspx

LIST OF ACRONYMS

ACRONYM	DEFINITION
AIS	Automatic Identification System
AMPS	Account Management Provisioning System
AOR	Area of Responsibility
ARPA	Automatic Radar Plotting Aid
ATON	Aids to Navigation
CE	Categorical Exclusion
CFR	Code of Federal Regulations
CHS	Canadian Hydrographic Service
CIC	Combat Information Center
CMC	Creative Map Corps
CO/OIC	Commanding Officer/Officer- in-Charge
COG	Course Over Ground
CONN	Conning Officer
CPA	Closest Point of Approach
DHS	Department of Homeland Security
DLA	Defense Logistics Agency
DNC	Digital Nautical Chart
DR	Dead Reckoning
DVD-ROM	Digital Versatile Disc – Read Only Memory
ECDIS	Electronic Chart Display and Information System
eNAV	Electronic Navigation
ENC	Electronic Navigational Chart
EP	Estimated Position
GPS	Global Positioning System
JQR	Job Qualification Requirements
IALA	International Association of Marine Aids to Navigation and Lighthouse Authorities
IENC	Inland Electronic Navigational Chart
IHO	International Hydrographic Organization
IMO	International Maritime Organization
LAN	Local Apparent Noon
LNM	Local Notice to Mariners
LOP	Line of Position
MOVREP	Movement Report
MTL	Master Training List
NARA	National Archives and Records Administration

ACRONYM	DEFINITION
NDGPS	Nationwide Differential Global Positioning System
NEPA	National Environmental Policy Act
NIST	National Institute of Standards and Technology
NGA	National Geospatial-Intelligence Agency
NOAA	National Oceanic and Atmospheric Administration
NM	Nautical Mile
NTM	Notice to Mariners
OOD	Officer of the Deck
OPORDER	Operations Order
POD	Print on Demand
PQS	Personnel Qualification Standard
RNC	Raster Navigational Chart
RPM	Revolutions Per Minute
SINS	Scalable Integrated Navigation System
SINS-II	Scalable Integrated Navigation System - Second Generation
SOG	Speed Over Ground
SOP	Standard Operation Procedures
STELLA	System To Estimate Latitude and Longitude Astronomically
TBD	To Be Determined
TTP	Tactics, Techniques and Procedures
UKHO	United Kingdom Hydrographic Office
USACE	United States Army Corps of Engineers
VTS	Vessel Traffic Service
WAAS	Wide Area Augmentation System
WAGB	U.S. Coast Guard Icebreaker
WIX	U.S. Coast Guard Training Barque Eagle
WHEC	U.S. Coast Guard High Endurance Cutter
WLB	U.S. Coast Guard Seagoing Buoy Tender
WMEC	U.S. Coast Guard Medium Endurance Cutter
WMSL	U.S. Coast Guard Maritime Security Cutter, Large
WMSM	U.S. Coast Guard Maritime Security Cutter Medium
WMSP	U.S. Coast Guard Maritime Security Cutter Polar
XO/XPO	Executive Officer/Executive Petty Officer
YDS	Yards

Table 1-A

ANCHORING

A. <u>General</u>. This Section states the basic requirements for anchoring. Ships must maintain navigational awareness while approaching an anchorage, while anchored, and while weighing anchor.

B. <u>Proficiency</u>.

  1. <u>Cutter Class</u>. All cutters must maintain proficiency in anchoring in accordance with Reference (b). Cutters can tailor anchoring drills to the specific capabilities of their class.

  2. <u>Requirements</u>. To be considered proficient, cutters must be able to:

     a. Prepare appropriate charts, plotting sheets, or eNav system for an anchorage.

     b. Determine appropriate anchorage area and bottom type.

     c. Approach an anchorage.

     d. Anchor the ship.

     e. Determine ship's position while at anchor.

     f. Weigh anchor.

  3. <u>Opportunities</u>. Weather and operations permitting, cutters must take advantage of opportunities to maintain proficiency in anchoring.

C. <u>Requirements</u>.

  1. <u>Documentation</u>. The Ship's Log must include time of anchorage, depth of water, which anchor used, scope of chain, type of bottom, ship's head, and bearings to objects designated by the Navigator. The anchor watch must use the ship's Standard Bearing Book (OPNAV 3530/2 or equivalent) to record time, vessel position, ship's head, bearings to objects designated by the Navigator, and depth of water.

  2. <u>Calculations</u>.

     > ***NOTE****: eNav systems may use more complex and accurate calculations for these definitions below, which will result in different distances than manual calculations described below.*

     a. The Letting Go Circle, centered on the anchoring location, has a radius equal to the distance from the hawsepipe to the pelorus, radar antenna, or GPS antenna.

     b. The Swing Circle, centered on the anchoring location, has a radius equal to length of the vessel added to the length of anchor chain released.

    c. The Drag Circle, centered on the anchoring location, has a radius equal to the distance from the hawsepipe to pelorus, radar antenna, or GPS antenna, added to the length of the anchor chain released.

3. <u>Navigation Team Responsibilities</u>. (In addition to responsibilities listed in Enclosure (4) of this document.)

    a. Determine Set and Drift as soon as possible when approaching the anchorage to account for it in course recommendations.

    b. As the anchor is let go, the navigation team must immediately mark a round of bearings, ranges, and record the ship's head.

    c. After plotting the fix, the navigation team must extend a line from the fix in the direction of the ship's head and mark hawsepipe to pelorus distance along the line, thus plotting the position of the anchor at the moment of letting go.

    d. The navigation team must continue to take fixes until it is determined the anchor is holding.

    e. Approved eNav systems feature various anchor dragging alarms and plotting options. Use these features (if equipped) in lieu of a paper chart/plotting sheet as long as the eNav system is fully operational.

    f. Command Navigation Standards must address specific anchoring procedures for the navigation team, including verifying position accuracy by other than primary means at regular intervals.

CELESTIAL NAVIGATION

A. <u>General</u>. This Section states the basic requirements for celestial navigation. Nothing in this Section relieves members of their responsibility to complete celestial navigation portions of Reference (f).

B. <u>Proficiency</u>.

   1. <u>Cutter Class</u>. WMSP, WAGB, WMSL, WHEC, WMSM, WMEC, WIX, and D14/D17 WLB class cutters must maintain proficiency in the art of celestial navigation.

   2. <u>Requirements</u>. To be considered proficient, cutters must be able to:

      a. Determine the time of sunrise, sunset, moonrise, moonset, and Local Apparent Noon (LAN).

      b. Determine gyro error by azimuth and amplitude of the sun or other celestial body.

      c. Obtain a LOP from the sun.

      d. Compute latitude by observing LAN.

      e. Obtain the ship's position by reducing celestial observations to a fix.

      f. Compute latitude and gyro error by Polaris.

   3. <u>Opportunities</u>. Weather and operations permitting, cutters must take advantage of opportunities to maintain proficiency in celestial navigation.

   4. <u>Training</u>. The unit Master Training List (MTL) identifies the personnel required to complete Celestial Navigation Training (course code 500940) to ensure proficiency as described in this Manual. At their discretion, Commanding Officers can require additional members to complete this training to ensure proficiency in celestial navigation.

C. <u>Other Requirements</u>.

   1. <u>Documentation</u>. Document all celestial work in the ship's Navigation Workbook (OPNAV 3530/1).

   2. <u>Computer Computations</u>. Units using the STELLA computer software application to perform celestial computations must follow the guidelines in Enclosure (9) to properly log the celestial sight information.

   3. <u>Chronometers</u>. There is no longer a requirement to carry chronometers onboard. Crews can obtain observation time(s) from an electronic clock synchronized with the GPS time signal or the National Institute of Standards and Technology (NIST) radio station WWVH broadcast. WWVH operates in the high frequency (HF) and broadcasts at 10,000W on 5 MHz, 10 MHz, and 15 MHz; and 2500W on 2.5 MHz and 20 MHz.

NAVIGATION TEAMS

A. <u>Boat Navigation Team Organization</u>. The Coxswain may assign navigation support functions to members of the boat crew. If the Coxswain decides to do this, then he or she must use the Bridge Navigation Team roles described in this Enclosure (modified as needed to address boat navigation capabilities and crewing). Combining roles may be necessary, depending on boat crew size. For example, the Coxswain can assign a crewmember as Helmsman and assign another crewmember as Plotter/Navigation Evaluator.

B. <u>Bridge Navigation Team Organization</u>. Bridge navigation teams must complete applicable Sections of Reference (f) and cutter specific job qualification requirements (JQR) for their assigned billets. Assign Navigation Team positions as appropriate for the method of navigation in use. The following are standard navigation team positions and duties:

   1. <u>Navigation Evaluator</u>. If not the Navigator, this person is responsible to the Navigator and must:

      a. Coordinate the actions of all bridge navigation team members.

      b. Use all available information to ensure the safe passage of the vessel including electronic fixes plotted on a paper chart, or displayed on an electronic navigation system.

      c. Evaluate fix accuracy from the Bridge and CIC (if equipped).

      d. Evaluate ship's projected movements.

      e. Make reports to the Conn as specified in the Command Navigation Standards.

      f. Ensure information displayed on eNav correlates to environment by visual verification.

   2. <u>Navigation Plotter</u>. The Navigation Plotter should not be the same individual as the Navigation Evaluator, unless there is a lack of available cutter personnel. The Navigation Plotter must maintain the navigation plot as follows:

      a. When using manual plotting methods:

         (1) Plot and label each fix on the chart in use.

         (2) Extend the DR at least two fix intervals.

         (3) Compute set and drift since last fix.

         (4) Identify nearest hazard to navigation.

         (5) Determine time and distance to the next course change.

         (6) Revise turn bearings.

         (7) Complete other tasks as directed by the Navigator/Navigation Evaluator.

      b. When using automated plotting:

(1) Plot various types of fixes as applicable, based on the installed electronic navigation system.

(2) Maintain best scale of chart and adjust chart view area to best match navigational picture.

(3) Complete other tasks as directed by the Navigator/Navigation Evaluator.

3. <u>Bearing Book Recorder</u>. When the cutter is navigating using manual plotting, the recorder must:

   a. Maintain the Standard Bearing Book (OPNAV 3530/2 or equivalent) in accordance with this Manual.

   b. Maintain communications with the Bearing Takers.

   c. Mark fixes at intervals specified by the Navigation Evaluator.

   d. Pass pertinent information to the Navigation Plotter/Navigation Evaluator.

4. <u>Bearing Takers</u>.

   a. Obtain accurate bearings to navigation aids designated by the Navigation Plotter/Navigation Evaluator.

   b. Advise the Navigation Plotter regarding the navigation aids available for use, including when navigation aids are acquired visually or lost from sight.

5. <u>Bridge Radar Observer</u>.

   a. Provide all radar navigation data as directed by the Navigation Plotter/Navigation Evaluator.

   b. Perform the duties of Navigation/Shipping Radar Operator on cutters without a CIC.

6. <u>Leadsman</u>. Pass soundings to the bridge navigation team for comparison with the fathometer and charted depth.

C. <u>CIC Navigation Team Organization</u>. (This Section only applies to CIC-equipped cutters.)

1. Cutters with a CIC must maintain a capability to stand up a secondary navigation team (i.e. CIC Navigation Team). When in use, the secondary navigation team should be ready to assume primary navigation team responsibilities.

2. Due to the configuration of WMSLs, the secondary navigation team is authorized to be placed on the bridge or other suitable location. WMSL Command Navigation Standards must specify the secondary navigation location.

3. COs may direct use of the CIC Navigation Team at their discretion. Normally, the CIC Navigation Team supports the Bridge Navigation Team in higher-risk evolutions (e.g., unfamiliar port transits, adverse environmental conditions, night/low visibility transits, transits with significant shipping traffic). The CIC Navigation Team verifies vessel position using methods such as radar ranges or radar chart matching, which contributes to the shipping picture and safe navigation of the vessel.

4. Command Navigation Standards must list conditions when the CIC Navigation Team is required.

5. CIC Navigation Team members must complete applicable Sections of Reference (f) and cutter specific JQR for their assigned billets.

6. On cutters without a CIC, some Sections of this PQS might apply to the Bridge Navigation Team (e.g., shipping officer, shipping radar operator).

7. The following are recommended CIC navigation team positions:

   a. <u>CIC Evaluator</u>. Provide recommendations to the Navigation Evaluator in regards to safe navigation of the vessel. The CIC Evaluator must:

      (1) Evaluate fix accuracy and the surface picture.

      (2) Make recommendations to the navigation evaluator based on CIC's navigation plot.

      (3) Verify that the recommended course is clear of all surface contacts.

   b. <u>CIC Navigation/Shipping Radar Operator</u>.

      (1) Provide all navigation radar data as directed by the CIC Evaluator.

      (2) Provide all shipping radar data as directed by the CIC Evaluator.

   c. <u>CIC Navigation Recorder</u>.

      (1) Record all ranges and/or bearings used by CIC for plotting fixes.

      (2) Assume responsibility from the Bearing Book Recorder for designating times of fixes when CIC has been designated as the primary navigation plot.

   d. <u>CIC Navigation Plotter</u>. Maintains CIC's paper plot (if applicable).

      (1) Plot and label each fix on the chart in use.

      (2) Extend the DR at least two fix intervals.

      (3) Compute set and drift since last fix.

      (4) Identify nearest hazard to navigation.

      (5) Determine time and distance to the next course change.

      (6) Revise turn bearings.

      (7) Complete other tasks as directed by the CIC Evaluator.

LINE HANDLING COMMANDS

This Enclosure provides a list of standard line handling commands to meet the requirements of this Manual.

COMMAND	ACTION
PUT OVER (line number)	Pass the specified line to the pier and provide enough slack to allow line handlers to place the line over the bit, cleat, or bollard.
HOLD (line number)	Do not let any more line out even though the risk of parting may exist.
CHECK (line number)	Hold heavy tension on the specified line but render it as necessary to prevent parting the line.
SURGE (line number)	Hold moderate tension on a line but render it enough to permit movement of the ship.
EASE (line number)	Let a line out until it is under less tension, but not slacked.
SLACK (line number)	Take all tension off a line.
TAKE THE SLACK OUT OF (line number)	Take all the slack out of a line, but do not take a strain.
SHIFT (line number)	Move a line to the specified location.
HEAVE AROUND ON (line number)	Take a strain on a line.
TAKE (line number) TO POWER	Take the specified line to the capstan or gypsy head and make ready to heave around (DO NOT heave around until told to do so).
SINGLE UP (line number)	Take in all but one bight so there remains a single part to the line. Can also be used to single up all normal mooring lines.
DOUBLE UP (line number)	Pass an additional bight on the specified line so there are three parts to the line. This can also be used to double up all normal mooring lines. Cutters without sufficient mooring line for three parts should just pass the bitter end of the single up to the pier.
AVAST or AVAST HEAVING (line number)	Stop taking a strain on a line with capstan.
CAST OFF (line number)	When using another ship's lines to secure your ship, it means to cast off the ends of their lines.
TAKE IN (line number)	Allow the pier line handler enough slack to take the line off the fitting and bring the line aboard. Used when secured with your own line.
STAND BY YOUR LINES	Man the lines, ready to cast off or moor.
BACK EASY	A command to the capstan operator to ease tension on the line once the stopper is passed. This command is given before up-behind.
UP-BEHIND	Cease hauling on the line and slack it quickly.

Table 5-A

1

HELM COMMANDS

This Enclosure provides a list of commonly used helm commands that units can tailor appropriately to meet the requirements of this Manual. Standard phraseology governing orders to the Helmsman is required to ensure the Helmsman understands and promptly executes all orders. The Helmsman must repeat each command word-for-word and must report when the ordered action is complete. The Conning Officer/Coxswain must acknowledge the Helmsman's responses with "VERY WELL."

__COMMAND__	__ACTION__
RIGHT (LEFT) STANDARD (FULL) RUDDER	Apply the ordered rudder. Standard rudder is the amount required to turn the ship on its standard tactical diameter. The rudder angle varies from ship to ship. Full rudder is normally the amount required for reduced tactical diameter.
RIGHT (LEFT) ## DEGREES RUDDER	Apply the ordered rudder. The Conn can follow this order with a new course for the Helmsman to steer, such as "STEADY ON COURSE 256" or another rudder command. If the Conn does not specify a course, the Helmsman must call out the heading at 10-degree increments, such as "PASSING 150, PASSING 160," until the Conn orders a course.
EASE YOUR RUDDER/EASE YOUR RUDDER TO RIGHT (LEFT) ## DEGREES	Decrease the rudder angle by half the amount currently applied or by the amount ordered. The Conn can follow this order with a new course for the Helmsman to steer or another rudder command. If the Conn does not specify a course, the Helmsman must call out the heading at 10-degree increments until the Conn orders a course.
RUDDER AMIDSHIPS	Place the rudder at zero degrees.
MEET HER	Use the rudder as necessary to check the swing of the ship without steadying on any specific course.
STEADY, STEADY AS SHE GOES, STEADY ON COURSE ###	Steer the course on which the ship is currently headed or the ordered course. If the ship is turning and the Conn gives the command STEADY or STEADY AS SHE GOES, the Helmsman notes the heading and brings the ship back to the heading. The Helmsman should then reply "STEADY; COURSE ###."
STEER ON	The Helmsman steers on a range or object identified by the Conning Officer.

COMMAND	**ACTION**
SHIFT YOUR RUDDER	Move the rudder to the same angle in the opposite direction from where it is currently ordered. The Conn can only give this order when a specific rudder angle is in effect.
NOTHING TO THE RIGHT (LEFT) OF COURSE ###	Steer nothing to the right (left) of the course specified.
HOW'S YOUR RUDDER	This is a query from the Conn to ascertain the current rudder placement. The Helmsman replies, "MY RUDDER IS RIGHT(LEFT) ## DEGREES."
MARK YOUR HEAD	A command to the Helmsman to state the heading of the ship at the moment the command was given. The Helmsman responds, "MARK ###."
COMMAND	The Helmsman's response to the Conn if he/she did not hear a command, misunderstood a command, or believes a command is improper.
SALLY YOUR RUDDER	Shifting back and forth between a set number of degrees of right and left rudder as ordered by the OOD.
MIND YOUR HELM	A command from the Conn, CO, OOD (if separate), or the Navigator to the Helmsman to pay closer attention to his/her steering.

Table 6-A

NAVIGATION PLOTTING SYMBOLS

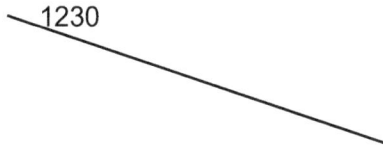

Single line of position
(Same for visual and electronic LOP)

Figure 7-A

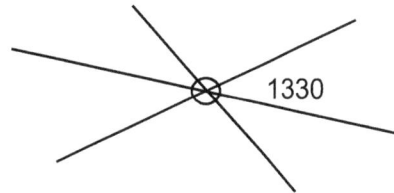

Visual fix

Figure 7-B

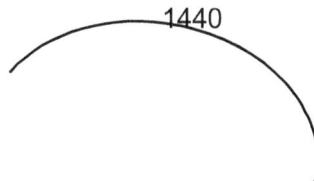

Distance arc or range

Figure 7-C

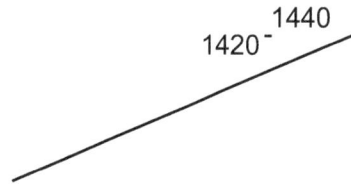

Advanced LOP
Original time and time LOP advanced to

Figure 7-D

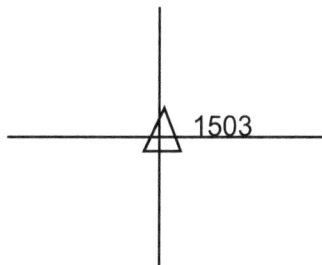

Electronic fix

Figure 7-E

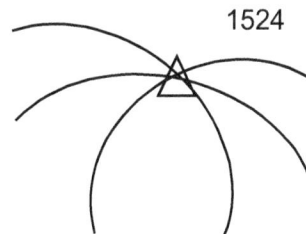

Electronic fix
using radar ranges

Figure 7-G

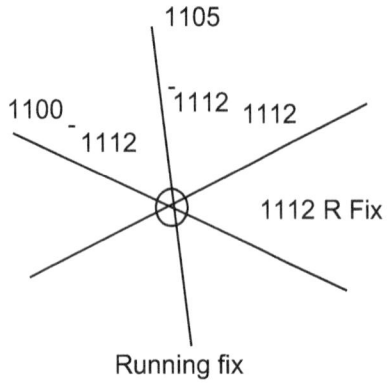

Running fix

Figure 7-H

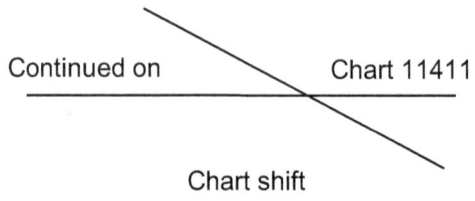

Chart shift

Figure 7-I

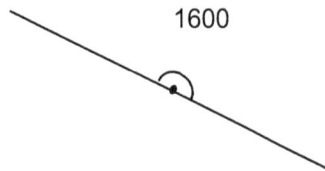

DR position.

Figure 7-J

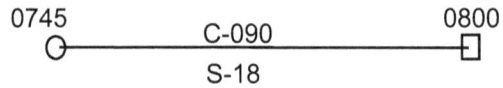

Actual course line
between a fix and an EP

Figure 7-K

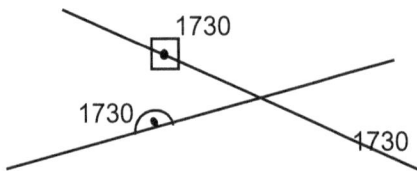

Estimated Position (EP) based
on DR position and single LOP

Figure 7-L

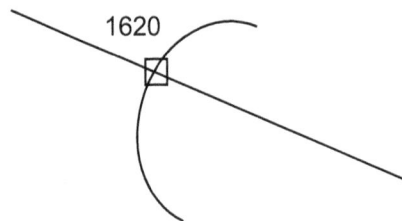

EP based on two LOPs.

Figure 7-M

C-090T / 087M
S-18.3 / D-17NM

WP1   WP2

1230   1245   1300

C-090
S-15

DR course line

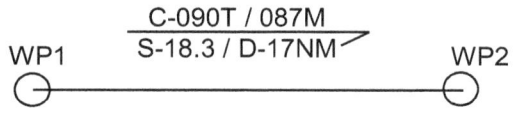

Trackline. Used
between intended waypoints.

Figure 7-N

Figure 7-O

1610

1715

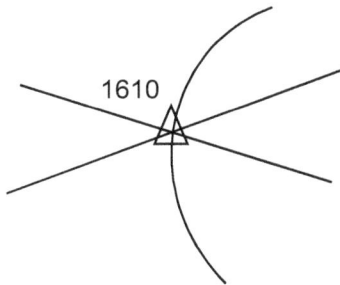

Two visual bearings
and one radar range

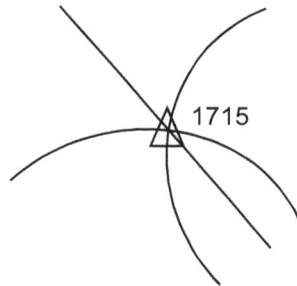

Two radar ranges
and one visual bearing.

Figure 7-P

Figure 7-Q

0730

0730   0745

C-090
S-15

0700   0715

0745

0745 R Fix   0800   C-090   0815
S-15

0730

0730 - 0745

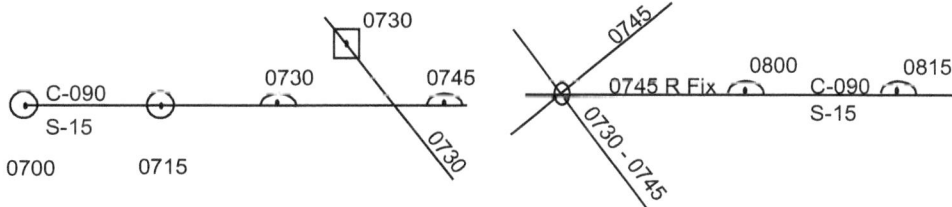

Examples of a DR course line with an EP and a DR course line with a running fix

Figure 7-R

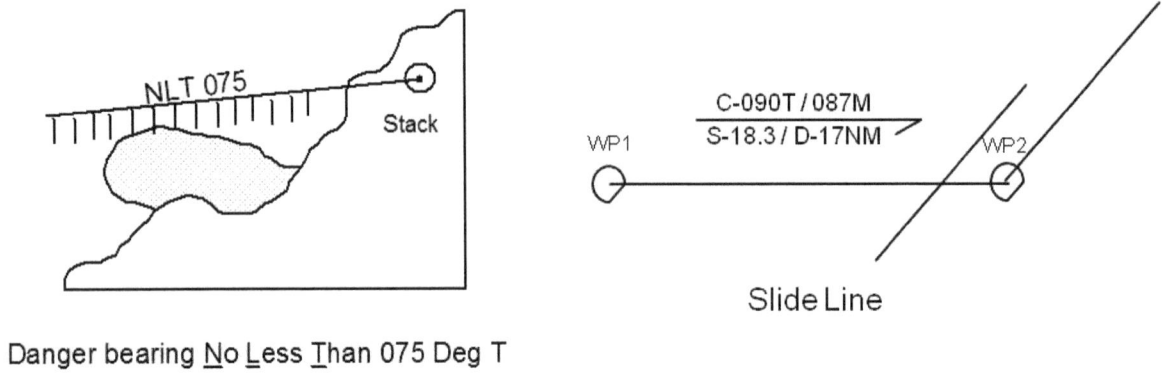

Danger bearing <u>No</u> <u>L</u>ess <u>T</u>han 075 Deg T

Slide Line

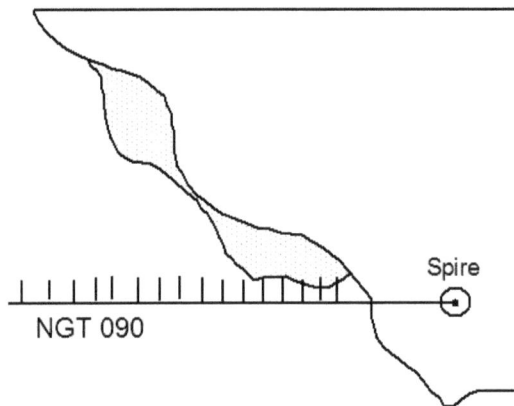

Danger bearing <u>No</u> <u>G</u>reater <u>T</u>han 090 Deg T

Figure 7-S

Marking of Visual and Radar Navigation Points		
Symbol	**Type of Aid**	**Highlighted Color**
	Visual Object – sequentially labeled V1, V2, V3, or VA,VB, VC, etc.	Yellow
	Radar Object – sequentially labeled R1, R2, R3, or RA, RB, RC, etc.	Orange
	Used for both (visual and radar) – sequentially labeled VR1, VR2, VR3, or VRA, VRB, VRC, etc.	Yellow and Orange

Table 7-A

GPS OUTAGE REPORTING

A. <u>General</u>. All Coast Guard GPS/NDGPS/WAAS users must adhere to the following:

B. <u>GPS and WAAS</u>. Units must report degradations, outages, and other incidents or anomalies to the Navigation Center via the GPS Problem Worksheet located at: http://www.navcen.uscg.gov/?pageName=gpsUserInput.

C. <u>NDGPS</u>. Units must report degradations, outages, and other incidents or anomalies at: http://www.navcen.uscg.gov/?pageName=dgpsUserInput.

D. <u>Connectivity Restricted Units</u>. Users must submit reports via priority message to COGARD NAVCEN ALEXANDRIA VA//NIS//.

1. GPS reports must contain the following information, if available:

   a. Start time of outage/anomaly.

   b. End time of outage/anomaly.

   c. Location where the outage/anomaly occurred.

   d. GPS user equipment make/mode.

   e. Elevation of GPS antenna.

   f. GPS frequencies (L1/L2) in use at time of outage/anomaly.

   g. Number of satellites the system was tracking at time of outage/anomaly.

   h. Which satellites the system was tracking at time of outage/anomaly.

   i. Summary (provide additional information, unusual screen display indicating problem).

   j. Point of contact.

2. NDGPS reports must contain the following information, if available:

   a. Start time of outage/anomaly.

   b. End time of outage/anomaly.

   c. Location where the outage/anomaly occurred.

   d. NDGPS user equipment make/mode.

   e. Elevation of NDGPS antenna.

   f. NDGPS beacon in use at time of outage/anomaly.

    g. Availability of standard positioning via GPS at time of outage/anomaly.

    h. Summary (provide additional information, unusual screen displays indicating problem, steps taken to troubleshoot/resolve).

    i. Point of contact.

3. WAAS reports must contain the following information, if available:

    a. Start time of outage/anomaly.

    b. End time of outage/anomaly.

    c. Location where the outage/anomaly occurred.

    d. WAAS user equipment make/mode.

    e. Elevation of WAAS-capable GPS antenna.

    f. Availability of standard positioning via GPS at time of outage/anomaly.

    g. Summary (provide additional information unusual screen displays indicating problem, steps taken to troubleshoot/resolve).

    h. Point of contact.

CUTTER LOGS AND RECORDS

A. <u>General</u>. This Section, in conjunction with References (i) and (j), outlines the procedures and requirements for maintaining navigational records. This Section provides guidance for the following logs and records.

    1. Log-Remarks Sheet, Form CG-4380A.

    2. Log-Weather Observation and Operational Summary Sheet, Form CG-4380B.

    3. Log-Navigation Data Sheet, Form CG-4380C.

    4. Deviation Table, Form CG-2596.

    5. Navy Navigation Workbook, OPNAV 3530/1.

    6. Standard Bearing Book, OPNAV 3530/2.

    7. Ship Position Log, OPNAV 3100/3.

    8. Combat Information Center (CIC) Navigation Log.

    9. Captain's Night Orders.

    10. Unit Checklists.

B. <u>OPNAV Logs/Workbooks</u>. The Navy Navigation Workbook, OPNAV-3530/1; Standard Bearing Book, OPNAV-3530/2; and Ship's Position Log, OPNAV-3100/3 are available through the Naval Forms Online website (https://forms.documentservices.dla.mil/process/). Registration and use of a government credit card is required. Once registered, conduct a search using the name or OPNAV number.

C. <u>Permanent and Temporary Records</u>. Cutter logs and records are official records and are either permanent or temporary records.

    1. <u>Permanent Records</u>. Log Remarks Sheet, Form CG-4380A and Log-Weather Observation and Operational Summary Sheet, Form CG-4380B are permanent records. Unit must retain, maintain, and permanently transfer these records to the appropriate Federal Records center in accordance with References (i) and (j).

    2. <u>Temporary Records</u>. All other logs and records listed above are temporary records. Units must maintain these records locally and dispose of them in accordance with this Manual and References (i) and (j).

D. <u>Electronic Logs and Records</u>.

    1. Units using an eNav system as their primary means of navigation are authorized to use the system's voyage-recording feature in lieu of Log-Navigation Data Sheet, Form CG-

4380C; Ship Position Log, OPNAV 3100/3; and Standard Bearing Book, OPNAV 3530/2 if the system records, at a minimum, the following information:

    a. Date/Time.

    b. Primary positioning source in use.

    c. Latitude/longitude position from primary positioning system.

    d. Course over ground (COG)/Speed over ground (SOG).

    e. True heading.

    f. Logged speed.

    g. Chart the system is using.

    h. Visual/radar objects and LOPs used (if applicable).

    i. Depth.

2. Compass Checks and Deviation Tables. If the cutter meets the requirements listed above, compass checks normally recorded in the Log-Navigation Data Sheet, Form CG-4380C are not required. These standards recommend that OODs verbally receive a compass check every half hour and on every course change. Cutters equipped with alternate heading sources, such as a fluxgate compass, are not required to post deviation tables, but they are required to ensure that the compasses and all remote repeaters are operating within the limits specified in the manufacturer's technical manuals. At a minimum, units must calibrate these compasses (in accordance with the manufacturer's instructions) annually and immediately following major maintenance availabilities and post deviation tables on the bridge. Record all calibrations in the unit's smooth log. Additionally, cutters equipped with a functional degaussing system that do not have an alternate heading source, must have deviation tables available for the use by the navigation team. Units should further check the compasses for accuracy before every underway period.

3. Maintenance.

    a. Save electronic navigation records locally on the system or on removable media. These may be deleted after three-years.

    b. Units storing records on removable media must ensure the records remain readable on the currently installed system throughout the three-year period.

E. Additional Guidance.

1. Deck Logs. Maintain Log Remarks Sheet, Form CG-4380A; Log-Weather Observation and Operational Summary Sheet, Form CG-4380B; and Log-Navigation Data Sheet, Form CG-4380C in accordance with Reference (j).

2. Navy Navigation Workbook, OPNAV 3530/1. This is a record of observations and computations for ship navigation, including celestial lines of position, tides, currents, and gyro error. In view of the large amount of data that users typically record, ships can

organize data into separate notebooks at the CO/OIC's discretion. The Navigator must review each computation and sign the workbook as appropriate. Maintain the workbook and all electronic records locally for three years after the date of the final entry, and then destroy them.

a. Computer Software. When using software for computations, units can print out and maintain the results with the navigation workbook or stored electronically in a retrievable format.

b. System to Estimate Latitude and Longitude Astronomically (STELLA). Units using STELLA software to perform celestial computations must print or save the STELLA navigation log after each celestial observation.

c. Strip Forms. If used, affix or record locally prepared strip forms in the workbook.

d. Calculator Use. If calculators are used, the user must record enough data in the workbook to reconstruct the computation.

3. Standard Bearing Book, OPNAV 3530/2 (or equivalent). This is a record of data that determines the ship's position, including visual bearings, sextant angles, radar ranges, and electronic LOPs. Maintain this book per the procedures below. Maintain this log locally for three years after the date of the final entry, and then destroy it.

a. Chart Number. Each day, record the chart number in use at the top of the initial page, and note each chart shift in the first available blank line.

b. Time Zone and Date. Indicate current time zone and date.

c. Radar Ranges. Label radar ranges YD (yards) or NM (nautical miles).

d. Soundings. Record soundings with each fix, and label them FT (feet), FM (fathoms), or M (meters).

e. Bearings. All bearings are true, unless otherwise indicated by R (relative) or M (magnetic). When shifting to relative, note the shift on the first available blank line, and record the ship's heading with each fix.

f. Abbreviations. All abbreviations must be in accordance with Nautical Chart Symbols, Abbreviations, and Terms, Chart No. 1.

g. Gyro/Radar Error. Record gyro error each day at the top of the initial page. Note any revised gyro error in the first available blank line. Enter radar range error, if determined, at the top of the initial page each day.

h. Navigation Aids. Crews must maintain a list of navigation aids in the bearing book or as part of a gazetteer with lists of charted objects for all piloting charts. The gazetteer must remain close to the plotting station for ready reference. Object lists must include the chart number, proper object name, latitude and longitude, and alphanumeric designation of the object. Object lists maintained in CIC and the Bridge must be identical.

    i. Signature. At the end of the watch or navigation detail, the bearing recorder must sign the Standard Bearing Book on the next available line.

4. Ship Position Log, OPNAV 3100/3 (or equivalent). A Ship Position Log is a record of latitude and longitude positions and soundings from all positioning sources. Use this log during coastal and open ocean navigation. If using visual bearings and radar ranges to determine the cutter's position, crews can secure the Ship Position Log and use the Standard Bearing Book. Maintain this log locally for three years after the date of the final entry, and then destroy it.

5. Combat Information Center (CIC) Navigation Log. The CIC Navigation Log is a record of data that determines the ship's position by radar when navigating on paper charts. When in use, CIC must maintain this log in accordance with the procedures described below. Maintain this log locally for three years after the date of the final entry, and then destroy it.

    a. Page Labeling. Enter the date, chart number, and gyro error at the top of each page. Note any revised gyro error in the log. Enter the radar range error, if determined, at the top of the initial page each day.

    b. Fix Recording. Record the following with every fix:

        (1) Identification of landmarks used.

        (2) Ship's position relative to track.

        (3) Recommended course and speed.

        (4) Nearest shoal water.

        (5) Distance to turn.

        (6) Time to turn.

        (7) Nearest aid to navigation.

        (8) Sounding at each fix, labeled FT (feet), FM (fathoms), or M (meters).

        (9) Set and drift (as required).

        (10) Any pertinent remarks (e.g., Conn does/does not concur).

    c. Securing the Log. When the navigation detail secures, make an entry on the next available line in the log. Draw a single line through the remainder of the page with the log keeper's signature on the line.

d. <u>Radar Ranges</u>. Record radar ranges in yards (YD) or nautical miles (NM).

e. <u>Abbreviations</u>. All abbreviations must be in accordance with U.S. Chart 1, Nautical Chart Symbols and Abbreviations, unless promulgated separately in the log.

f. <u>Navigation Aids</u>. Requirements are the same as those described above in Paragraph E.3.h of this Enclosure.

6. <u>Captain's Night Orders</u>. Units have traditionally maintained the Captain's Night Orders Book in a bound ledger or in loose-leaf form. The CO writes and signs the orders for each night as Reference (a) requires. They include such items as courses and speeds to maintain throughout the night, expected sightings, engineering data, the tactical situation, and supplementary orders to the OOD. Instead of paper orders, CO/OICs can use electronic media to convey night orders to the crew. With either option, units must institute safeguards to ensure that Deck Watch Officers and other key personnel acknowledge the orders. Classified Nightly Battle Orders are optional and used in addition to Night Orders if the tactical situation warrants. Maintain these orders locally for three years after the date of the final entry, and then destroy them.

> ***NOTE***: *Reference (a) requires that units keep a night order book containing standing orders and all other orders affecting the navigation and operation of the vessel.*

7. <u>Checklists</u>. Per Enclosures (10) and (11), cutters must create, maintain, and complete checklists for getting underway and entering port/restricted waters. Maintain these completed checklists locally for 30 days and then destroy them.

8. <u>Record Retention</u>. Per Reference (j), and regardless of any authorization contained in this Manual, do not destroy records that directly relate to the following matters until after final clearance or settlement:

a. <u>Claim</u>. An outstanding claim for or against the United States.

b. <u>Litigation</u>. A case under litigation.

c. <u>Investigation</u>. An incomplete investigation.

SAMPLE CUTTER GETTING UNDERWAY CHECKLIST

This Enclosure provides a sample checklist containing common actions that units must take prior to getting underway. Units can tailor this checklist as appropriate to ensure safe navigation of the vessel.

<u>**Time prior to**</u>	<u>**Event**</u>
TBD by CO/OIC	Make a voyage plan.
48 Hours	Establish getting underway schedule covering: propulsion plant light off, shift from shore to cutter power, disposal of cutter vehicles, light off and testing of electronic suite, U.S. and Guard Mail dispatch and receipt.
	Release Movement Report (MOVREP).
24 Hours	Conduct navigation brief.
	Finalize Deliberate Risk Management Plan and brief CO/OIC.
	Verify arrangements for tugs/pilots/line handlers.
	Verify schedule for lighting-off power plant.
	Energize gyrocompasses.
	Check navigation lights for proper operation (Preferably at night).
	Ascertain schedule of other vessel movements in harbor on underway day.
4 Hours	Energize all radars except those prohibited by local electromagnetic emissions restrictions.
	Energize and configure eNav system, if so equipped.
	Validate accuracy of alternate heading source if so equipped.
	Validate NDGPS/GPS datum.
	Reconfirm tugs/pilots/line handlers.
	Verify arrangements for terminating shore services.
	Verify removal of floats, barges, containment booms.
2 Hours	Ascertain from the XO/XPO any anticipated deviations from the Plan of the Day.
	Promulgate underway time to all hands.
	Energize and initialize all electronic navigation equipment. (Coordinate with shift from shore to cutter power.)
	Energize and calibrate all radar repeaters. (Post errors at each repeater and for navigation plotters.)

Determine and post gyro, steering, and navigation repeater errors and enter into electronic navigation system, as applicable. Check/energize all other electronic equipment (e.g., fathometer, radar, etc.).

Conduct radio checks on all required circuits (include bridge-to-bridge radiotelephone).

1 Hour   Conduct Real-Time Risk Assessment via GAR 2.0 Afloat Risk Assessment form.

Set Material Condition Yoke.

Tune and optimize radars.

Post tide/current/aids to navigation information on the bridge and CIC.

45 Minutes   Fix ship's position using all available positioning sources.

Record draft of cutter fore and aft in cutter's deck log.

30 Minutes   Station the Special Sea Detail and/or Anchor Detail.

In reduced visibility:

1. Station the low visibility detail.

2. Set material condition Zebra on main deck and below.

Embark pilot. Display CODE HOTEL.

Check steering in all available modes.

Test sound-powered phone circuits in use.

Receive department reports for readiness to get underway.

Test anchor windlass.

Prepare anchor(s) for letting go.

OOD shift watch to the bridge.

15 Minutes   Obtain CO/OICs permission to shift to pilot house control (when equipped) and test main engine(s).

Direct engineering control accordingly after ensuring that the screw(s) are clear.

Test cutter's whistle/general alarms.

Single up lines.

Make SECURITE calls.

Take in the brow and break all shore connections.

Conduct time check.

Report when "ready for getting underway" to the XO/XPO.

10 Minutes   Notify engineering control to standby to answer all bells or of impending pilothouse control maneuvers.

	Set Special Sea Detail and/or Mooring Stations.
	Conduct Risk Assessment (Real Time).
Underway	Shift colors.
	Close up international call sign (if appropriate).
	Establish radio guard.
	Make SECURITE calls.
	Report underway to VTS if appropriate.
After U/W	Return checklist to Navigator for filing.

SAMPLE CUTTER ENTERING PORT/APPROACHING RESTRICTED WATERS CHECKLIST

This Enclosure provides a sample checklist containing common actions that units must take prior to Entering Port/Approaching Restricted Waters. This checklist is an example, and units can tailor it to match the circumstances of the navigational situation and to ensure safe navigation of the vessel.

Time prior to   **Event**

TBD by CO/OIC Conduct navigation brief.

3 Hours   Determine and post gyro, steering, and navigation repeater errors and enter into electronic navigation system, as applicable.

1 Hour   Conduct Real-Time Risk Assessment via GAR 2.0 Afloat Risk Assessment form.

Pass the word, "Make all preparations for entering port. Cutter will anchor (berth _____ side to) at about _____. All hands shift into the Uniform of the Day."

Lay out mooring lines if required.

Set up and monitor all harbor and tug radio frequencies.

Check into VTS when appropriate.

Ascertain schedule of other vessel movements in harbor.

45 Minutes   Test cutter's whistle/general alarms.

Prior to approaching restricted waters, check steering in all available modes.

Test backing bells.

Hoist international call sign when entering inland waters (if applicable).

30 Minutes   Station Navigation Detail

Station the Special Sea Detail and Anchor Detail.

Make anchor(s) ready for use.

Inform the Anchor Detail of depth of water at anchorage, type of bottom, ready anchor, and scope of chain to be used.

Inform First Lieutenant as to range of tide and time of high water.

Receive readiness reports for entering port.

Make SECURITE calls.

Request permission to enter port from the proper authority.

15 Minutes   If mooring to a buoy, lower boat with buoy detail as directed.

Station line handlers.

Upon Mooring   Secure main engines on _____ hour standby.

Secure gyros and navigational radars as directed.

Check out of VTS as appropriate.

Secure radio guard.

If anchored, obtain navigation bearings and ranges, and determine swing and drag circles.

Record draft of cutter fore and aft.

Shift watch to quarterdeck.

Return checklist to Navigator for filing.

Release arrival MOVREP.

VOYAGE PLANNING REFERENCES AND RESOURCES

All nautical publications are available on NGA's Digital Nautical Publications-Quarterly Update DVD-ROM (NGA Reference No.: CDPUBQTLY). All units are on an automatic distribution for the Quarterly Update and publications are currently corrected as of the production date of the DVD. When updates occur, units must apply corrections to the NGA copies or download updated publications.

When preparing charts and developing navigation or crew briefs, consult currently corrected nautical and hydrographic publications and information (printed or electronic equivalents). These sources are available via the NAVCEN website at https://www.navcen.uscg.gov or via the links provided below.

A. Coast Pilot* (available on the NOAA website at: https://nauticalcharts.noaa.gov/publications/coast-pilot/index.html. NOAA updates Coast Pilots weekly and posts the updates along with a complete edition containing all applicable corrections).

B. Fleet Guides.*

C. Sailing Directions* (available on the NGA website at: http://msi.nga.mil/NGAPortal/MSI.portal).

D. Code of Federal Regulations, Title 33 (available on the Government Publishing Office website at: http://www.ecfr.gov/).

   - 33 CFR 147 – Safety Zones
   - 33 CFR 161 – Vessel Traffic Management
   - 33 CFR 165 – Regulated Navigation Areas and Limited Access Areas.
   - 33 CFR 166 – Shipping Safety Fairways
   - 33 CFR 167 – Offshore Traffic Separation Schemes

E. Operations Order (OPORD).

F. Coast Guard Navigation Center, Navigation Information Service (see the Navigation Center's website at: http://www.navcen.uscg.gov/ for more information).

G. Naval Operating Area Instructions.

H. Light List(s) and List of Lights* (Light Lists are available on the Navigation Center's website at: http://www.navcen.uscg.gov/?pageName=lightLists with weekly updates at: http://www.navcen.uscg.gov/?pageName=lightListWeeklyUpdates. Light Lists and List of Lights are also available on the NGA website at: http://msi.nga.mil/NGAPortal/MSI.portal).

I. Radio Aids to Navigation, PUB 117* (available on the NGA website at: http://msi.nga.mil/NGAPortal/MSI.portal).

J. Notices to Mariners, Local Notices to Mariners, Broadcast Notices to Mariners, and Notices to shipping, as applicable (see the Navigation Center's website at: http://www.navcen.uscg.gov/?pageName=lnmMain for more information).

K. NAVAREA, HYDROLANT, HYDROPAC Messages (available on the NGA website at: http://msi.nga.mil/NGAPortal/MSI.portal).

L. Tide Tables* (available on the NOAA website at: https://tidesandcurrents.noaa.gov/).

M. Tidal Current Tables* (available on the NOAA website at: https://tidesandcurrents.noaa.gov/).

N. Nautical Almanac.

O. International Regulations for Preventing Collisions at Sea, 1972 COLREGS/Inland Navigation Rules (33 CFR 83) (previously referred to as Navigation Rules Handbook).

P. World Port Index* (available on the NGA website at: http://msi.nga.mil/NGAPortal/MSI.portal).

Q. Army Corp of Engineers port/channel survey data.

R. Local weather resources.

S. Other local navigation guides.

NOTE: * *Units may request hard copy from Government Printing Office.*

BOAT/CUTTER BOAT NAVIGATION KIT OUTFIT LIST

The following items are listed as required or optional for the boat/cutter boat navigation kit outfit. Part numbers are suggested, but alternatives are authorized.

Required Boat Navigation Kit Items:	QTY	Part Number:
Penlight with red lens	1EA	01HS22872 (Red lens)
Stopwatch with second hand or digital	1EA	13873 001260286
Parallel Ruler	1EA	81348 001911508
Parallel Plotter (weems)	1EA	49268 015569178
Divider/Compass with spare lead	2EA	49268 015569406
Course & Leg Identifier for SAR	1EA	49268 015522931
Nautical Slide Rule	1EA	49268 003911110
China Marker	as needed	81348 002401525
Gum Eraser	2EA	73685 003238788
Notepad	1EA	83421 014534585
Pencil Sharpening Pad	1EA	80244 002374926
#2 Pencils	as needed	N/A
Pencil Sharpener	1EA	N/A
Charts, Local AOR	Set	N/A
Required Cutter Boat Navigation Kit Items:	**QTY**	**Part Number:**
Penlight with red lens	1EA	01HS22872 (Red lens)
Stop Watch with second hand or digital	1EA	13873 001260286
Course & Leg Identifier for SAR	1EA	49268 015522931
Notepad	as needed	83421 014534585
#2 Pencils	as needed	N/A
Most Current and Up-to-Date Publications Required: (Electronic or Paper)	**QTY**	**Part Number:**
U.S. Coast Pilot for AOR (Optional for cutter boats)	1EA	N/A
Optional Items:	**QTY**	**Part Number:**
Navigation Kit Bag/Protective Case Equivalent	1 EA	14234958
Operator's Manual	1EA	N/A
Anemometer	1EA	58502 Davis Instruments P/N: 00271
Hand Held Compass	1EA	N/A
Flash Light	1EA	N/A
Dry Erase Markers	as needed	N/A
Pens	as needed	N/A

Table 13-A

www.ingramcontent.com/pod-product-compliance
Lightning Source LLC
Chambersburg PA
CBHW050620110426
42813CB00010B/2622